OUTSIDER

Paul Cullen is a journalist and the author of three previous non-fiction books. Born in London, he grew up in Dublin, where he studied engineering at Trinity College Dublin. He lived in Switzerland for five years before returning to Ireland to study journalism at Dublin City University. Appointed to *The Irish Times* in 1993, he reported on health, politics, consumer affairs, international development and education in a career spanning three decades. He wrote the bestselling book *With a Little Help from My Friends* about the planning tribunal's investigations into corruption. He has won many awards for his work, including Irish news journalist of the year in 2023. He is married, with four children, and lives in Dublin.

Also by Paul Cullen

Insider's Guide to Dublin, Wicklow and the Boyne Valley

Refugees and Asylum-Seekers in Ireland

With a Little Help from My Friends: Planning Corruption in Ireland

OUTSIDER

SURVIVAL, FAMILY SECRETS AND THE SEARCH TO BELONG

PAUL CULLEN

HACHETTE
BOOKS
IRELAND

Copyright © 2026 Paul Cullen

The right of Paul Cullen to be identified as the author of the work has been asserted by him in accordance with the Copyright, Designs and Patents Act 1988.

First published in Ireland in 2026 by HACHETTE BOOKS IRELAND

1

All rights reserved. No part of this publication may be reproduced, stored in a retrieval system, or transmitted, in any form or by any means without the prior written permission of the publisher, nor be otherwise circulated in any form of binding or cover other than that in which it is published and without a similar condition being imposed on the subsequent purchaser.

Cataloguing in Publication Data is available from the British Library.

ISBN 9781399755863

Typeset in Sabon LT Std by Bookends Publishing Services, Dublin.
Printed and bound in Great Britain by Clays Ltd, Elcograf S.p.A.

Lines from Mark Roper's poem 'After the Fall', from his collection *Bindweed* (2017), are reproduced by kind permission of Dedalus Press.

Hachette Books Ireland policy is to use papers that are natural, renewable and recyclable products and made from wood grown in sustainable forests. The logging and manufacturing processes are expected to conform to the environmental regulations of the country of origin.

Hachette Books Ireland
8 Castlecourt Centre
Castleknock
Dublin 15
Ireland
(info@hbgi.ie)

Authorised representative in the EEA

A division of Hachette UK Ltd
Carmelite House, 50 Victoria Embankment, London EC4Y 0DZ

www.hachettebooksireland.ie

To Dee, Ella, Rosa, Tana and Luca

Author's Note

To protect their privacy, the names of my birth mother and foster mother, and any family members, have been changed.

In this book I have used the term 'birth mother' throughout, though I know that it has its critics. I did so for reasons of clarity and consistency, and because this was the term most often used as I was growing up to describe the woman who bore me.

I am afraid he will prove an awful handful.
—An adoption worker, referring to one-year-old me

What came from my mouth
was not word but bawl –
as I think now
of pain of course,
but also triumph –
Still here! Still here!
—from 'After the Fall' by Mark Roper

Prologue

7 October 2017

Uh-oh.

This is not good.

Here I am, in the centre of Europe, 3,000 metres above sea level. And about to plunge down a snow-covered mountain gully.

This can't end well. But before all the bad stuff, my life ripped apart and all that, a strange thing happens. Time shuts down. My mind takes a step back from my body. I get to observe my own predicament, suspended above the snowy wastes.

I sneak a glance at one hand, then the other. Both are detached from any connection to solid earth, both pawing the air uselessly. Stretching in front of them, a solid steel cable that represents safety if I can grab it but is, sadly, just out of reach.

And there, below me, are my feet, dangling, useless. Now it hits me: I am about to plummet into the icy wastes below.

The moment is a cartoon that has replayed in my mind ever since. In it, somehow, I am watching someone else's drama, rather than playing the lead role in my own. A curiously familiar feeling.

All too soon, the illusion ends. The frame in the cartoon unfreezes. I begin to slide down Zugspitze, Germany's highest peak.

I fall feet first down the precipitous mountain, belly and face thrust into the snow, lathered in spindrift. Splaying hands and arms, I try desperately to arrest my plunge. With all the force I can muster, I ram the toe caps of my boots into the mountain. Kick, kick, kick!

My efforts bear fruit. I slalom across the slope, losing speed. Muscles burn painfully as I dig in even harder. Slower again. Now I can ease off. I allow myself a relieved exhalation, through clenched teeth.

Alas, the respite is short-lived. In one smooth movement I sail over a lip on the slope and am flipped onto my back. The gradient steepens sharply. I take off down the slope once more. This time, gravity brooks no dissent. The mountain is merciless, tossing me from hummock to hummock like a projectile in a pinball machine. Thunk, thunk, thunk, I bounce across its high flanks.

While my body is being thrown about, my mind remains oddly clear. I relinquish hope. There is a time for everything under the heavens, I tell myself, even a time to die. Mountains like these take no prisoners. Gravity will dictate the pace of my slide down the gully. I will gain speed even as I lose altitude. Farther down, the snow will thin out, exposing the rocks beneath. Inevitably, I will be flung onto these boulders and smashed to bits. The end will be bloody – and quick.

I resolve to accept my fate. Random thoughts flit through my mind, mere flickers of brain activity. I give thanks for the beautiful day I have just enjoyed: the precious hours spent with old school friends, until the moment of my fall; the life I have led up to now; my wife and children.

But there is a darker hue to my mind's wandering. A sense of something missing, or incomplete. A job not done; a question left unanswered. It's like that dream of falling you wake up from – only this time I *am* falling. No thoughts I have time to put my finger on, just a question: who exactly is this happening to?

Suddenly, the unexpected. My movement slows. The terrain has flattened out. A vertical cliff-face to my left jerks back into focus. With one exhausted effort, I force my heels down into the snow and lurch to a tentative halt.

Silence. I lie crumpled on the snow. Random quips and song-titles flit through my disordered mind. Well now, what fresh hell is this? There must be some way out of here. That's another fine mess you've got me into. I laugh mirthlessly.

Enough. I am conscious, stationary. I can move my fingers and toes, even lift my head. Wriggling from side to side, I manage to shuck off my backpack and lever my mobile phone out of a pocket. The screen is blank, the battery dead.

There is an emergency whistle in the pocket. I blow it without strength or conviction. I am too far away from anyone to be heard.

As my breathing slows, pain rises up within me. Something is wrong. Something is broken inside me.

I don't want to dwell on it. I need to be positive.

I am not dead. And – the thought strikes me with remarkable clarity – I will not die.

Well, probably not.

My fall started in Germany. By now, I may well be in Austria. Perhaps my left side rests in one country and my right rests in the other. It does not matter. Things work in this part of the world. Yes, I tell myself, I *will* be rescued. If help arrives soon enough. If the cold doesn't get me first. Yes, I will see my family again.

All I have to do is wait. And as I lie here, I think about my life, and what I have made of it. If I get to enjoy more, what will I do with it? I think about my beginnings, those questions that have been lurking beneath the surface for so long. Who am I? Where did I come from? Where was I in those unrecorded early years before I was adopted?

It's a lot to take in, what with the shock, the pain and the uncertainty. And yet I know I shall never feel time as keenly as I feel it now, in this awful moment. I may be teetering on the brink of existence but I sense every second as precious. I resolve to use each one wisely, to order my thoughts.

Dusk is approaching. The light is draining out of the day,

any remaining heat too. Another night's freeze is setting in. As the pain worsens, I keen softly in the snow. It is well below freezing now.

As my body starts to shiver, my mind teems with thoughts. I have been in scrapes before. My life has been a procession through the cat's nine lives. On every occasion, I came out unscathed. Not this time. Even if I survive this, I am likely to pay a big price. There won't be any more lives to use up if I get out of here. There may not be any life worth living.

Enough self-pity. Amid the gloom, my thoughts are more real than they have been for years. How I love life! I want so much to survive, to go back to my old existence with family and friends. But I know everything has changed with this Saturday afternoon calamity. I daren't think of returning to normality after this, pretending nothing is different. I daren't shirk the questions that have been lurking just beneath the surface for so long.

As I have up to now. There isn't time now for the detail – weariness is spreading over me – but I tell myself I will face those questions and answer them. Things will have to change. But first I need to get out of here alive.

I find myself sliding again, a few inches at first, then slightly faster. By digging my heels into the snow, I manage to come to a halt again.

Lying inert and helpless on the freezing slope of the mountain, all warmth ebbs out of me. The snow greys as the sun slides behind the mountain. The valley is readying itself for the desolation of night. Yet I cling still to hope from the sky, still faintly blue, so vast above my petty predicament.

I yearn to sleep, because sleep will bring rest and make me forget what has just happened. I might dream myself back in time, before this mess occurred. Back even farther, to the start of my life, where the mystery began. But sleep is dangerous, I know. I might not return from it.

So I try to shuffle my arms and legs, the working bits of me. I am a small child once more, creating an angel in the snow that no-one can see.

1

I am adopted. This is the central fact of my life, one I have been running away from for so long. Yes, I have always known about the *fact* of my adoption, along with a few sketchy details of how I was shunted hither and thither as a tiny baby. But even now, decades later, I know so little about where I came from. And what happened to me after I was born. Not just for minutes and hours, but for months and years.

I am the jigsaw with missing pieces, yet I have done all I can to avoid completing the puzzle. Now I ask: how can I know where I am going without knowing where I started?

I know what I have achieved. Despite those mysteries of my early years and the undoubted jolt of adoption, I flourished. Blessed with the love of others, I built a successful career and a happy family. I had a life.

Yet I have lived that life in denial. Something has always been lacking. Rootedness, a proper sense of myself. An ability to live in the moment, to take satisfaction from my accomplishments. At times, an emptiness as vast as the mountain on which I now find myself, all warmth slowly seeping out of me.

Over time, this perception has got worse, not better. I have tried to quell the doubts, to tell myself that I am just like everyone else. But I am not. I look and talk like others. To look at me, I am just another middle-aged dad, pushing swings and driving teenagers around. I head to work in the morning and return each evening. On the face of it, I am an insider in society, a journalist for a national newspaper, the numbers of government ministers and celebrities on my mobile.

Yet that is not how it feels to me here, now, at the sharp end of existence. At the core of my identity, my understanding of who I am, is a void. Owing to my fractured past, I feel like an outsider.

Finally, I know it is time for me to put the pieces together, to make sense of it all. The irony isn't lost on me – the dawning has come as I stare death in the face.

2

My mother is expecting to adopt a newborn, fragile and quiescent and malleable. Instead, she gets me.

It is September 1965 and, at age two years and four months, I arrive in my new home a stomping, fully formed toddler. I look as if I have taken a short cut through a sweet shop, or overdosed on infant formula. Coarse-featured, said the doctor. Huge, really gross, exclaimed the social worker. Gauche, big, loose-looking, she added for good measure. Likely to be an awful handful.

Relatives and neighbours turn up, expecting a cute baby they can dandle and hug, not the bawling terror who has been dragged through the door. Behold my red and raw bottom, my dowdy, worn-out clothes. The tattered little sandals on my feet, which have been painted and repainted with varnish to make them last longer. The enamel stripped from my rotting baby teeth, which will soon require extraction under general anaesthetic.

There is so much more to my eventful short life, but the adults present are strangers to me. If they only knew – the constant crying, the persistent bronchial infections, the chickenpox, the measles, the hole in my heart. It is a wonder I have made it here at all.

The lady who drove me here, I remember her from before. I am certain she could tell them all about me, where I have been. But this woman, a social worker, has left already with her secrets, out the door with her serious face after the cup of tea that was offered. Prising my tiny fingers out of her skirt as she makes to leave, pushing me towards the small, dark-haired woman with the terrified look on her face. Mary, your new mammy. And, beside her on the settee, say hello to Patrick, your daddy. At least he is smiling, unruly eyebrows peeping up above black spectacles.

I start the visit upset, and stay that way for the entire day. No words, just roars and screams, audible on the street outside. God love him, the people say. Poor mite. Who are you people? I want to say. Where has my mammy gone? Why are you not calling me by my proper name?

Exhaustion, finally. 'Patrick put you on his lap and you buried your curly locks in his chest as you cried your heart out,' according to Teresa, my first cousin once removed. 'There you stayed. You couldn't be moved. We didn't know what to do. Poor Patrick couldn't even get his jacket off. Eventually, he went off to lie on the bed with you still on his chest, and had to sleep the night in his clothes.'

Finding my voice the next morning. 'Mammy gone,' I wail over and over again, crying for four days straight. Around the garden I run, searching behind the yellow privet hedge and among the rhubarb stools for 'my other mammy'. Mary watching me from the kitchen sink, sucking on a Carrolls Number 1; Patrick out working, not seen until evening time.

After two weeks, the social worker comes again. Mary whispers to her at the kitchen table, while I play with blocks in the corner. The lady makes notes in her book. *Hands full. End of her tether. Nerves gone. Needs vitamins.*

I keep my eye on this lady all the time, afraid she might disappear like my other mammy. In bed that night, I wake up crying, another nightmare where I'm looking high and low for my mammy. Mary and Patrick arrive together to comfort me and change the wet sheets.

The lady visits again, and then another time too. The two women talk in low voices, but I can make out some words: *All fine. Settled.* The lady is smiling broadly as she takes her bag and leaves.

Except that she arrives yet again the following week, and this time Mary is doing the crying. *Told a fib, I'm very sorry. Afraid you might take him away from us. Like this from the start. Just can't do it.*

Suddenly, Mary has an idea, she tells the lady. The spell must be broken. Turning to me: 'Would you like to go back to where you came from? Do you want your other mammy?'

'Yes!'

Yes yes, I say, bobbing around the room. Gathering my toys immediately and putting them into a plastic shopping bag.

But Mary is crying again, even harder than before. What have I done? I do not want to hurt her. I only wanted to find my mammy.

The lady is shaking her head. She stands up, turns to me, hands on hips. 'No. That's enough now.'

Both of us shocked out of our jiggering and crying.

The lady turns to Mary. 'Never mind the fierce temper on him, it will pass.'

The force of her voice. My little bag crumples to the ground. Sobs rise up within me, wave after wave. I am going nowhere.

Time does pass. Things settle down, as the social worker predicted. I take on a new first name – Paul – as well as a second name – Cullen. I go to the shop with Mary each day for an ice-cream. When a dog scares me on the street, it is her leg I clutch. The road outside is packed with children of all ages, whose games I join. I make friends with another Paul, who is my age and lives nearby.

One Sunday, when he is not working, Patrick gets down on his hands and knees and tells me to climb onto his back. Up I clamber, and the two of us lumber around on the swirly patterned carpet, him making horsey sounds and me yelling. Faster, faster! Faster, Daddy! For the first time, I laugh.

3

High above me, two hawks circle in the thermals, the last rays of sun illuminating their plumage. How tiny and insignificant I am in this vast, white arena. I am shaking, increasingly fearful of the approaching dark. Help cannot come soon enough.

Despair is setting in, a feeling that my race has been run. My breathing is growing shallow. The earth's chill is rising up within me, dulling pain but also the will to live. I cease bothering to raise my head and scan the skyline.

And then the silence is broken. A low sonic boom bounces around the valley, the unmistakable sound of a helicopter. I count on my fingers as the whup-whup of my potential saviour nears: one-two-three-four-five, the rotors still thrumming up from the valley floor; six-seven-eight-nine-ten, and the bellowing mechanical beast soars abruptly into view. In no time, it is hovering over the gully where I lie. I wave frantically, shouting uselessly amid the din. No need; one of the crew signals with a thumbs-up that he has spotted me.

The helicopter circles a few times, its pilot evidently sizing up the terrain. Darkness is falling but there is still enough light to work by. I will him to land quickly but he holds his height. He must think it is not safe to descend beside me.

The door of the cabin slides open and a man in a bright red jumpsuit emerges. The man clips himself into some sort of harness, which the pilot lowers slowly to the ground. Landing just a few metres away from me, he unclips himself.

The man walks over to me and lowers himself gently by my side. He shouts something in German that I cannot make out above the racket, then whispers in my ear. Now I can hear his beautiful words: 'My name is Daniel. I am going to save you.'

Accidents happen in a second, recoveries last a lifetime.

My journey back from the abyss begins with Daniel attaching himself to me using the harness. I am brought from the horizontal to the vertical. Hugging me tightly, he signals with a spiralling gesture for the pilot to ascend. I am drifting in and out of consciousness by now, no longer sure what is happening. With my likely injuries, I know, he cannot risk moving me too much.

The helicopter lifts off into the sky, the two of us swinging from a rescue cable below the cabin. Initially, the pilot flies out horizontally from the mountain and we soar into pure air like trapeze artists suspended on a wire. Travelling at a constant altitude, he tracks the line of the valley below. We sway along underneath him, our distance from the ground increasing as the terrain falls away. The earth beneath us changes in colour from white to black, as snow is succeeded farther down the mountain by ominous, dark rocks – the rocks I might have clattered into had my slide gone on. Despite all that has happened, I am stunned by the view.

The pilot banks left and descends towards the wide floor of a valley. In the distance, an ambulance is waiting for us in the misting twilight. The helicopter lands on solid, snow-free ground, now thankfully flat again. From the vehicle, a trio of manly paramedics, all moustaches and bright uniforms, materialises. One man unclips me, then lays me flat on a stretcher. Daniel and his colleagues push me through the open doors of the ambulance and get to work.

It is clear they have done this often before. The four of them are operating in a confined space, but each man moves with quiet efficiency, cutting away my garments, attaching an oxygen mask to my face and a drip to my arm, treating my surface injuries and prodding me with gloved fingers for internal damage.

I remain conscious and alert throughout, answering the questions fired at me, babbling a bit. One of the team, on hearing I am Irish, tells me he has just seen U2 play in Berlin. Within minutes, I am returned to the Red Cross helicopter, this time securely strapped to a gurney in the cabin. The pilot takes off again over the lights of middle Europe, flying north, away from the fateful mountains. There is talk in the cockpit of heading to the hospital in Garmisch, a town I know from skiing trips. The painkillers take effect. I drift off to sleep.

I come to in a hospital bed, the room bathed in warm fluorescent light. Multiple tubes and wires run from my body to the medical equipment around the bed. Monitors blink and beep. My old school-friends, my companions for this weekend away, are standing at the back of the room. All of them, thankfully; two had taken a cable-car to the top but one, I remember now, was standing beside me as I fell. He got safely to the top with the help of other climbers but suffered frostbite in his finger-tips.

The sun has gone down and come up again since my accident. It is Sunday, the end of the weekend. My friends are telling me almost shyly that they need to go home. I am not going anywhere.

After they leave, a doctor tells me about my injuries, but it is hard to take anything in. In my head, I am replaying the exact moment when I missed a hold, clawed the air and lost contact with the mountain. Over and over, it plays out, this cartoon clip I cannot stop.

The accident happened at the end of a long day's walking, just under the 2,962-metre peak of Zugspitze. I slid more than 150 metres down the slope, the medic is telling me. There are broken bones, collapsed lungs, multiple wounds and bruises, the effects of hypothermia. The fall caused a catastrophic break in my spine, rendering it highly unstable. Emergency surgery was the only option, he explains.

The doctor is brisk and matter-of-fact. Though the medical team operated on me immediately, and are happy with their work, he thinks a further operation might be required. They have inserted a rod in my back, secured in place with titanium screws, where the vertebra had burst. With luck, my spinal cord will remain unaffected, he tells me, smiling as he heads out the door.

I drift back to sleep, under heavy sedation. The nightmare re-enactment of the exact moment I fell continues to play in my dreams. A simple misjudgement: a misplaced hand; end-of-day fatigue and the effects of high altitude, perhaps. Again and again, I can't help thinking: what if?

When I wake, it is evening, or so the staff tell me. I am stable enough to be wheeled down a corridor to a recovery ward, with numerous medical supply lines for company. I ask the nurse how the skiing is in Garmisch, but she gives me a blank look. We aren't in Garmisch, the nearest hospital to Zugspitze, it turns out. Because of the severity of my injuries, she explains, the helicopter pilot was directed to fly farther north, to Murnau, an hour south-west of Munich. There I was deposited at a regional trauma clinic, specialising in complex back surgery. This, for now, is my home.

I lie and sleep and wake and think and sleep again. It feels like I am lying with a block under my spine. The pain is getting to me. My emotions are a jumble. Relief at surviving. Anger at my stupidity. Guilt at the impact on others. Fear for the future. Questions, hovering.

A phone is put to my ear. Dee. My wife had been driving around Dublin, buying shoes for the children, when she got the news. The message was staccato. 'Are you driving? Pull over,' said one of my walking friends. He and another of our foursome had taken the cable car to the panoramic restaurant at the top of the mountain and they had, with the other customers, witnessed my fall with horror. Then I slid from their view. The outcome of my fall was unknown, though some stranger in the restaurant who witnessed the accident declared to all present that I was 'a goner'. 'Paul fell down the mountain,' my friend told a silent Dee. 'A helicopter came and we think they got him, but we don't know where they brought him.' Long pause. 'Or if he's alive.'

After that call, an hour passed, maybe two. She went home and made a cake. Said nothing to the children. The delay, the lack of clear information, was excruciating. She didn't call anyone else, she said, because she wouldn't have known what she was telling them. Eventually, further details dribbled across Europe: I was 'responsive'. Her not-dead, or not-yet-dead, husband had been found. His condition was unknown. Better, but so many bleak outcomes still possible.

More hours passed. More news trickled home – about my late-night flight to Murnau, followed by the emergency operation – before it became clear I would survive.

Our conversation is brief, fitful. One moment, I am sobbing hard into the phone; the next, I have drifted off under the influence of the morphine.

The following day, the surgeons appear. Good news, they say. The surgery has been a success. No second procedure will be needed. They show me scans of my spine and its new metal insert. The head of the team predicts a full recovery, then moves on to the next patient, his work done.

Between the bouts of pain and sedation, I am elated. I have cheated death and, I hope, disability. The nurses hand me an information sheet that sets out a generic road map for recovery in cases like mine. From the seventh week, it says in black and white, I can resume sports. 'Cross-country skiing, cycling, jogging, hiking, swimming and Nordic walking' are permitted. No vibrations or load-bearing for my spine for the next three months, but all activities allowed after that.

I cannot look at the sheet often enough. By Christmas, I should be able to resume my normal life. It is barely believable.

The physiotherapist pays a visit. She encourages me to sit up in the bed. It is an effort but I can do it. I want to do it. I want to get better as soon as possible.

The next day she brings a walking frame. I take my first halting steps. I can't go far from the bed because I am still hooked up to so many tubes. These, I am told, will be removed one by one over the days to come.

The physiotherapist arrives again the following morning. Unhooking my tubes, she leads me and a portable drip for a shuffle down the corridor. It is three days since my operation. Again, I manage it, one tiny, feeble step at a time. But that evening my legs are on fire. The pain is excruciating. I plead with the nurses for painkillers. It is the first indication that my recovery will not be straightforward; that the battering my body took was more comprehensive than the doctors assumed; that complex injuries entail a complex recovery.

I sleep by day and lie awake at night. Often, it is the discomfort that keeps me awake; at other times, the tubes running awkwardly under my back. But I am also restless. I think of the questions that reared up when I was lying on the snow, waiting to be rescued. Where did I come from? What have I made of myself? What now? Why have I never wondered about these perfectly obvious things before?

For the first time in years, I have the space and time to think. I reflect on the promise I made, lying on the mountain, to make sense of my life, to find the missing pieces. We are all the sum of our experiences, and yet I do not know what those experiences were for me in my earliest years. My book is missing its first chapter; my words begin mid-sentence.

I can't sleep, so I take to dictating my thoughts onto my mobile phone under the covers. But I'm half-sedated and more than a little morose, so the recording I listen back to the next day sounds like a self-help book. *I need to move forward, I need to fix myself up, which I can do, but I also need to analyse, just get it out of my head to understand how on earth this happened to me*, I tell myself.

Always busy, always challenging myself, but where has that got me? *I seem to be attracted to risk, to danger. Where did that come from? What does it say about my relationship to everyday, normal life?*

An overwhelming sense of loss floods over me, but this is not a new feeling. I have experienced it in darker moments over the years. It is time to be honest with myself, to own up to a truth I had begun to intuit in recent years but had not yet acknowledged. Now I understand the reason: it is the pain of not knowing who I am.

4

Mam is in one of her moods again. I'm only eight years old, but I've become good at avoiding her when she gets like this. Not today, though. She nabs me when I'm dodging out the front door to play on the road.

'I know what you've done. I know you've been on to them.'

'I – I don't know what you're saying. What are you talking about?'

'You've been talking to that lady in the agency. Looking for your other mother. I know it; I can see from the look of you.'

My cheeks redden, though what she is saying makes no sense to me. It isn't true. 'Honest to God, Mam, I haven't. Sure how would I, even if I wanted to? We don't even have a phone.'

'The devil finds ways. Haven't I seen the car?'

Although I have no notion what she's talking about, I still manage to sound guilty as I stammer a response.

'What do you mean – what car?'

'Your mother. In a big fancy car. I've seen her. Outside our house. Waiting. Spying on us, the hussy. Up to no good.'

Had my birth mother really turned up outside our house? Why would she do that? It didn't sound possible, but I didn't know for sure. But if Mam said this had happened, surely she was right?

'Really, I know nothing about this. I haven't seen anyone. Even if she was there, nobody told me.'

Heading up to sleep, I can't resist a peek out the landing window. Holding my breath, scanning the road outside. No car. A feeling of relief that things will stay the same. But disappointment, too.

Lying captive on the hospital bed, my mind is a busy train station of thoughts bustling in from far in the past and departing again. From early childhood, I never questioned my adopted status within the family. I never nourished the thought that my life could have been lived somewhere else. Initially, I never thought very much about the woman who bore me – referred to at home as 'your other mother' or, awkwardly, often bitterly, 'your "real" mother'.

My avoidance of the subject was a survival tactic to help me deal with my mother's roller coaster emotions. But it took years for me to realise this.

My parents were deeply insecure about my adoption. They had an irrational fear I could be taken from them in the blink of an eye. They found it difficult to broach the subject of my origins. And they probably didn't want to be reminded of their prior childlessness.

My mother came up with bizarre strategies for coping with this imagined threat. On her good days, she told me hyped-up versions of my origin story, fairy tales populated with the kind of successful professionals she might have liked to become herself.

'Your real mam was a beautiful woman, with long black wavy hair,' she told me once. 'She was a true beauty.'

I looked at her quizzically. I had not asked for this information, which popped out of her while we were on a walk. A minute earlier, we had been looking for the dog, who had disappeared into the bushes that bordered the factory grounds at the end of our road.

'She was making a career for herself and then she fell head over heels for this fine, strong man.'

She wouldn't look at me when she told these stories. Today, her eyes were fixed on the greenery in the distance, though she wasn't that bothered where the dog was. When she got this way, she became sad.

'They were very much in love. But her parents were dead set against it. They wouldn't hear of her giving up her career for this man. And then you came along. They were doomed.'

I had questions, but some I knew better than to ask. Like the nuts and bolts of how I had 'come along'. Still, I couldn't resist nit-picking.

'But how could you know this? Didn't you say the adoption agency wouldn't tell you anything?'

'Ah, yes. Officially.' Mam tapped her nose with her finger. 'But I have ways ... The lady pulled me aside one day, and filled me in. She told me the whole story.'

'How were they doomed? Did something happen to them?'

She tapped her nose again, and sighed. 'I can't say much, I'm sworn to secrecy.'

That queer look again. Lady, our Jack Russell had emerged finally from the undergrowth, an old tennis ball in her mouth, looking pleased. Mam continued to ignore her.

'Just ... a car crash,' she sniffled. 'They didn't survive, the poor things. You were left an orphan.'

I was confused. This wasn't the first time Mam had told me these stories. But they were never the same.

'Your father – he was a professor at the university, a *very* important man,' I recalled her telling me a year earlier. 'And your mother, she was a beautiful doctor. They were very much in love. But then you were in her tummy. And they just weren't ready.'

I wondered too about the tummy business, but my mother moved the story on quickly. 'That's why it took so long for you to be adopted, love. They wanted to find the right family. It had to be the best for you. They knew you were special, so they searched and searched. It ended only when they found the perfect couple.'

'You? You and Dad?'

Mam, missing the note of incredulity in my response, didn't answer. Her eyes had misted up. She was lost in her thoughts.

Something darker took hold of her as I got older. The fairy tales were dispensed with in favour of direct accusations, delivered out of the blue. A form of madness gripped her, as she took to accusing me of hiding information or secretly trying to contact my birth mother.

On the street, she told anyone who would listen we were the spitting image of each other. It worked when I was a small child; less so as I grew to tower over her.

She often reminded me that I was free to contact 'her' once I turned eighteen. But what if I were to do this? I felt she was goading me into tracing my origins, so she could turn on me when I did.

5

The clinic moves me to a recovery ward, and I start eating solid food again. Dee flies over and brings fresh clothes, books and a semblance of normality. I am able to sit up briefly, unaided. Friends start sending me messages, wishing me well. Boxes of chocolates and get-well cards arrive.

My mood lifts. Though I am going through some long, dark nights of the soul, I have hit upon the nub of my worries: my sense of difference, a hole at the core of my being. It feels good to finally have the time to run the rule over myself.

Physically, I make steady progress. Each day, I travel farther with the walking frame, then dispense with it. I begin light exercises to rebuild my strength. I venture up and then down steps. I huff and puff to the entrance of the hospital and breathe in the sharp freshness of late autumn. The tubes and bags attached to my body disappear. My appetite returns. One night, my neighbour in the ward, another survivor of a bad accident, produces a bottle of local wine. Giddy with the medication we are on and a sense that things will get better, we fill tumblers and toast our precious lives.

The hospital is comfortable and spacious, a welcoming world of its own. Friends living in Germany come to visit. I spend long periods sitting outside on a balcony, gazing at the mountains where I came to grief. The late autumn weather is warm and sunny, an astonishing clarity to the light. I can hear, but not see, children playing happily in a wooded glen below. I feel the absence of my own children as an ache, as profound as any suffered by my body on the mountain.

All day, I watch the parasails in the distance drifting on the thermals rolling off the mountains. The screech of motorcyclists on their big bikes taking hairpin bends regularly reaches my balcony. I wonder whether any of these adventurers, too, will have a mishap, or worse. (That week, a young woman is rushed to the clinic with catastrophic injuries. She survives, but her spinal cord was crushed when her parasail crashed.)

After ten days, the surgeons say I am on the road to recovery. I can leave. I am not considered strong enough to sit up for the time it takes to travel home normally, so I will require a medical evacuation. Staff at my health insurer are helpful, but the flight home takes time to organise. Finally, I get the call to say a place has been booked for me on a scheduled flight from Munich to Dublin on the coming weekend. I weep uncontrollably, tears welling up out of some place I didn't know existed. I am the happiest man alive. After two weeks, I am going home.

On the day of travel, a paramedic arrives to accompany me on the journey. I will travel to the airport by ambulance. On the plane, I will be laid out on a stretcher, over rows of standard seats. Not my choice of homecoming, but then I have no choice. As we are leaving the clinic, I insist that I do not need help, that I am well enough to sit up on a chair in the ambulance. But the pain is too severe. I have to lie down again on a stretcher.

There are further complications at the airport. Ireland had experienced the tail-end of a hurricane while I was in hospital in Germany. A bumpy flight is expected in the storm's aftermath. The pilot refuses to take me on board without guarantees that he will not be liable for any injuries I suffer during the trip. To my embarrassment, the plane and its passengers stay stubbornly on the tarmac while efforts are made to sort out the issue. I am kept on a bed in a loading unit beside the plane while phone calls ping across Europe between insurers, medics and airline companies. Eventually, my health insurer agrees to accept liability. Staff load me onto the plane like gold bullion. The other passengers gaze at me with vacant curiosity. I don't have the energy to feel humiliated.

In Dublin, I am transferred to an ambulance hovering near the runway, where there is more waiting while passport formalities are completed. Eventually, cleared by immigration, we set off into the evening traffic. At last, I arrive home to a warm fire, a relieved family and a determination to dig into my past.

I spend the early weeks of recovery in bed, reading nineteenth-century novels between naps, big books I would never normally have time for. Rising for short periods, I move gingerly about the house and do a few easy chores. My strength starts to return. Soon I am able to go for brief walks outside. We get a dog.

As my body begins to come together again physically, I double down on my pledge to recompose myself mentally. Something good has to come out of this misfortune.

I resolve to address the unanswered questions of my early years. In truth, these are not unanswered questions, as I studiously refused to pose them for many years. While most adopted people want to know as much as possible about the circumstances of their adoption, a significant minority profess not to be curious. For many years, I was one of these.

Mostly, this was out of loyalty to my adoptive parents. Mary and Pat Cullen gave me a stable upbringing. To even venture down the path of inquiring into my birth parents felt like a betrayal, dangerous too. I convinced myself I was just too busy to deal with all that messy business from the past.

Millions of people have been adopted across the world, and each of their experiences is different. Yet all adoptees are, in some sense, misfits. As writer and adoptee Jeanette Winterson has written, adoption 'drops you into the story after it has started. It's like reading a book with the first few pages missing. It's like arriving after curtain up. The feeling that something is missing never ever leaves you – and it can't, and it shouldn't, because something is missing.'

We have lost our birth parents, even as our birth parents have suffered their own losses. We look the same as everyone else. We all get on with our lives, with varying degrees of success. But we are also *expected* to get on with our lives, to feel grateful to have escaped an early life in institutional care. All of which suits society because no-one wants to be reminded that children were abandoned, or mistreated.

I had started to look into my background in my thirties, initiated by contact from my birth mother. But then I ran into obstacles; the wall of secrecy around my adoption was a high one. Now, fresh from the shock of my accident, I was determined to learn more. But I also had questions about my upbringing. This was happy for the most part, but there were also periods of intense trauma.

And what about the wider legacy of adoption? More than 45,000 people have been adopted in Ireland since it was put on a legal footing in 1952. Almost as many were informally boarded out in the decades before then. Thus, hundreds of thousands of people have been directly affected by adoption, as children, birth parents, adoptive parents or wider family members.

There are still thousands of us adoptees hidden in plain sight across Ireland. All of us were compelled to take part in a giant experiment designed to preserve and protect the social conventions around marriage that prevailed at the time we were born. Few of us have been asked since whether that experiment worked. Now, with adoption having fallen out of favour, we linger on as uncomfortable reminders of a discredited era.

The fact of my adoption was known, to me and others, but most of the details were not. Secrecy was the hallmark of nearly all adoptions that took place in Ireland in the twentieth century.

Somehow I had come into the world in England but ended up in Ireland, growing up in a Dublin suburb. More questions that needed answering tumbled in after being ignored for so many years. There was the strange move I made between two countries. The circumstances of my adoption. Why did it take so long? Who was my birth father? Where did I spend those early years, before I was placed with a family? Who cared for me? How was I treated?

Most of all, I fretted all these years later: was I loved?

6

I can see every inch of the house in which I grew up – every dint in the wallpaper, every swirl in the pattern of the Tintawn carpet, every gewgaw gathering dust on the dining-room shelves. The clarity of my recall extends to the streets outside. The precise curve and elevation of kerbs we bounced balls off. The exact state of disrepair of the white picket fence at the end of the road that served as our tennis net when Wimbledon was on the telly. There, I see the spot where I hit Mr Fortune with a mis-thrown frisbee; here, which of Mrs Reilly's windows was broken by the football I punted from the road one idle day.

While the first three years of my life were a blank, memories were laid down thick and fast thereafter. My new home was a three-bedroom semi in a quiet cul-de-sac in south Dublin, the address hinting at the tenor of the times. Marian Grove, and the rest of the Marian estate where we lived, was named for the mother of Jesus Christ. The cult of Mary loomed large throughout my childhood. It was my mother's name, of course. The Blessed Virgin Mary was venerated on numerous religious feast days. There was no ill that could not be cured by the recital of a few Hail Marys. Her image adorned the wall calendars we used to mark the passage of the days. There was even a framed picture of the BVM in our sitting room. I used to imagine her watching the television with the rest of us, her face a perfect oval surrounded by a circle of stars, her lips pursed disapprovingly at this intrusion of modernity into family life.

Many years hence, these streets would go upmarket. Houses would be extended and driveways would fill up with fancy cars. But as I was growing up, the local men were solidly blue-collar, the women almost exclusively homemakers, proud to call themselves housewives.

Only a few families had cars, and they were bangers. There were barmen, milkmen, builders, fitters, mechanics and painters living on our street, along with a few office clerks. Most of our neighbours were freshly up from the country, with large families. The only exception was our next-door neighbour. He was a bachelor, a Corkman, a university graduate and an engineer with Dublin Corporation – all of which made the poor man a figure of suspicion for some of the neighbours.

Our house had a red Sacred Heart lamp glimmering day and night in the hall, beneath a framed picture of Jesus on the cross. Every day, my mother topped up the plastic holy water font by the door – another image of the Virgin Mary here – and reminded me to bless myself as I left the house.

The kitchen, reached directly from the hall via a door that opened out, was small and dark, a pity since so much time was spent there. A fluorescent tube hummed malevolently through dinner-time silences, casting a yellowish pallor on the room. This part of the house smelled permanently of tea and burnt toast in the morning; sausage and black pudding at tea-time. Dinner was in the middle of the day.

There was a good room to the front with table and chairs, which we used for eating Christmas dinner and little else. The adjacent sitting room, where we gathered most often, features in my earliest memory. In it, I am a small child wandering through the house while the adults drink tea in the kitchen. A fire in the grate casts flickering shadows on the walls of the sitting room, drawing me in. There are swirling orange patterns on the walls and brown swirls, going the other way, on the settee. The carpet feels scratchy under my bare feet. I jump at the sound of the carriage clock chiming loudly for the hour.

Beside the clock, on the mantelpiece, I spot a piece of paper, coloured a brilliant orange. I reach up on my tippy-toes, and pull down the paper – a ten-shilling banknote. It bears the image of a pretty woman wearing a hood, looking sideways over her shoulder. Her eyes track my gaze as I rotate the note left and right in my hands. Suddenly I am seized by a notion: this must be my other mother, the woman I have been told about. As I hold the note up to the fire, going closer and closer to the heat, she seems to be *in* the paper, not just on it. Brighter and brighter she looms before me as I bend towards the flames. She is still there, even brighter and hotter, when I turn the note over.

Suddenly, the note is whipped out of my hand, leaving me too shocked to cry. A firm hand, hairy and big and paint-flecked, pulls me back from the fire, up into warm arms. 'We don't want to lose Lady Lavery,' Dad says, 'or you.'

Of the three bedrooms upstairs, the one to the front was seldom used. Mam put up Spanish language students here every summer to bring in some money, until she tired of their hair oil on her settee and their aversion to Irish cuisine. Relatives stayed too, but there was some sort of row and they stopped coming. Thereafter, the room lay empty.

The largest bedroom, to the rear, was occupied by my parents. I rarely entered this gloomy space, except when one of them was sick. Like the time Dad got shingles, just when I was given a present of tickets for the Christmas panto. 'We could go without him' – Mam, sitting with his tray on the candlewick bedspread, plucking at unseen threads and making a sad face at me – 'or we could wait until he gets better, and then go.' Ever anxious to please, I made the decision she wanted me to make. But Dad took months to recover, the tickets were cashed in and I never got to go to the panto.

Mine was the box bedroom, also at the back, where in spring, birds bathed noisily in the gutter above and in summer the walls cracked in the heat of the morning sun. In winter, with two exposed walls facing east and north and no heating, it was an ice box, so cold that I disappeared for months under a mound of blankets. As I grew into a gangly teenager, Dad tacked a length of foam on a board and slotted it onto the end of the bed to support my protruding feet. I would always be too long for most beds.

The house had a long east-facing back garden bounded at the far end by a giant hedge of whitethorn and privet. This was where my parents spent their free time, tending to their roses and hydrangeas and forever trying to cultivate new crops, with mixed results. Though I had no green fingers, here was where I learned a slew of exotic words. I rolled the sounds around my mouth: cauliflower, kohlrabi, artichoke, rhubarb, blight.

To the side of the house was a garage accessed by an up-and-over metal door that always gave trouble. There, in all seasons, Dad mixed his paints at an ancient, stained table in one corner, battered tin cans and exotically labelled bottles arranged about him. In winter, he lit a SuperSer gas heater that barely banished the cold.

I spent long hours here with my father, inhaling the acrid smells from the freshly opened tins, watching him combine his colours with Monet-like care. He was a painter and decorator, just like his brothers and his father, and his grandfather, as well as a signwriter and specialist in graining, the art of using paint to recreate the look of wood, which was popular in the 1960s and 1970s.

I grew to love the vocabulary of his trade, another clutch of peculiar words driving my imagination – scumble, distemper, Swarfega, linseed, turpentine, shellac, putty, varnish. And more magical sounds in the many pigments he used: vermilion, sienna, ultramarine, umber, vandyke.

Once the day's work was out of the way, Dad lingered on in his man-shed to tinker with various projects. He built furniture for the house. He created toys for me – cricket stumps, a kite, a chessboard, a periscope, a go-kart fashioned from old pram parts and discarded pallets. He made crosses for the graves of local children who had died prematurely. The nuns from nearby Loreto Abbey wrote to thank him for his work renovating a religious statue. 'Enclosing £1 to buy yourself tobacco,' the mother superior told him in a brief note, 'the [rosary] beads is blessed.'

Most evenings, his labours complete, Dad planted himself on the settee and fell asleep in front of the telly. Watching him there, dozing in his open-necked shirt, his glasses having fallen to his lap, I wondered at this man who had chosen to be my father. Cautious, careworn, unquestioningly committed to rearing me; were all dads like this? Or were there other dads out there – mine, even – who flew to the moon, boxed for the heavyweight championship of the world, scored the winning goal for Leeds United in the FA Cup final? Who brimmed with confidence and cut a swathe through the world? Who held a pen, not a brush?

While he gently snored, Mam and I watched the news from the other end of the settee. None of the women on the television looked, or spoke, like my mother. None of them wore cardigans or headscarves or sensible slippers. They may have had wrinkles but it was hard to tell in black and white.

I finished my night-time biscuit and glass of milk as slowly as possible, not wanting to go to bed, not wanting to confront the darkness there.

No amount of pleading could defeat Mam's order for me to head upstairs, though. Once I had brushed my teeth, she came up to tuck me in. A quick kiss on the forehead, and my bedside light was extinguished. I was alone.

In the gloom, I lay there. This was my home. This was my family. I saw it all from above, floating high, unmoored, at a remove from everyone. My parents, moving about in the house I knew so well. Neighbours, bustling up and down the local roads. Myself, longer and leaner, all puppy fat fully fallen away, running around with my pals. And there, at the edge of my vision, the lady who had brought me here, leaving, growing smaller, fading from view.

It wasn't the content of the vision that bothered me, but the distance at which it unfurled. How I was of this world now, but not in it. How events unfolded before me, not to me. It was thrilling, but also unsettling, to see my life from such a distance, to be living vicariously. Observing myself, the seed of difference germinating within.

7

Ready? Deep breath then.
Ten –

The room is so sparsely furnished it must be rented. Only the chatter of birds through the roof window breaks the silence.

Nine –

The man sitting opposite me, his voice dropping to a steady whisper, is just a few years younger than me. He is casually dressed in a check shirt and runners, not what I expected. But then it is a warm spring day.

Eight –

He asks me to calm my thoughts. I try to comply, but struggle. Is that the tang of the sea filtering into the room? Have I locked the car? A swim after, for sure. But did I bring togs?

Seven –

The man is counting backwards. Between the numbers, he describes his method in a low voice. I am about to enter a deep trance, he says, and in that quiet space the two of us will explore my earlier life, the time I don't remember.

Six –

Six. Months have passed since my accident. I'm doing okay.

But I'm more frustrated than ever at the barriers I'm facing in unlocking the truth of my origins.

Five –

What if the answers are within you, a friend suggested. What if you don't have to rely on others to unlock your secrets? What if they could be freed through hypnosis?

Four –

Which is how I find myself sitting with a therapist. He says my mind will empty now of all thoughts as I pass deeper into a trance. I start to feel so tired. Despite myself, my thoughts are making themselves scarce.

Three –

The man tells me to put my hands out in front of me, on my thighs, with my fingers showing. They hang so heavy now, I can barely lift them.

Two –

He wants me to wiggle my little fingers in answer to his questions. Left pinkie means 'no', right pinkie means 'yes'. Or is it left means 'yes' and right means 'no'?

One –

Have I got that? Have I? I feel leaden; speaking, even thinking, feels too much for me. The present dissolves. My thoughts go where he takes them.

The hypnotherapist counted forwards now, reversing me out of the trance. The birds still chinwagging, somewhere high above. The modest warmth of an Irish spring still wafting through the windows. The bare room again. Back to the here and now.

Ninety minutes went by, according to the man, though I remembered nothing of it. For the first time in my life, I was under hypnosis. I did respond to some of the man's early questions by wiggling my small fingers, he said, but it wasn't easy. More often I failed to answer, so he had to pose questions in more basic forms to get some kind of response. He said that I seemed reluctant to go back in time. It was difficult for him to obtain clear information.

His biggest challenge was to get me to venture further back from my childhood into my infancy. It was as if a wall was in place separating these memories from more recent ones, he said. Neither had I any recollection of the time I arrived at my adoptive parents' house, and the events that directly followed.

I had a difficult time after being separated from my birth mother, he ventured, but I probably did not suffer major trauma. But he could not be more specific.

I wasn't that disappointed. My expectations were low anyway. How could this man, talented or no, elicit information without my even knowing it? Hypnotherapy was worth a try, but there weren't going to be any short cuts to connect me with my hidden past.

'Without families you don't get stories.'

Book therapy is a big part of my recuperation. Reading *The Cut Out Girl*, the tale of a young Jewish girl who was moved between different safe houses in The Netherlands during the

Second World War to avoid deportation to a Nazi death camp, the first line jumps out at me. In the chaos of war, all records and memories of Lien de Jong's earliest years were lost. For Lien and author Bart van Es, the role of stories is to ensure continuity and to help people make sense of themselves.

I too had no known family during my first years of existence; there are no stories of me from that time. And while there are surely records of mine gathering dust in some office, as an adoptee these have been largely beyond my reach. My official remembered existence began at age three.

I was too young to have memories from that period of upheaval, to compensate for the lack of eye-witness accounts of my upbringing. How many times have I wished that some shard of recollection from that distant past had stayed with me? The sight of dust-motes dancing in the sunlight above my cot, maybe. The deep, satisfying suck of a baby's bottle. A dollop of ice-cream licked off an adult's finger.

At least my amnesia was not selective. I was able to remember neither a joyous roll on a mattress with another infant nor a cut across the back of my legs for being bold. My lack of recall was comprehensive. I didn't know if I was in a home or with a family. On my own, or with other children. Was I well treated? I had no idea.

Slowly, in the weeks after the accident, my body began to heal. I came off all medication and started exercising gently. I still felt fragile, but was anxious to push myself. I was keen too to return to work, to return to normal, but everyone advised me to give myself time to recover. I didn't really need to be told this; as a health journalist, I knew well how the body keeps the score. My work as health editor of *The Irish Times* was sedentary; I was prone to spending hours hunched over a laptop when a deadline loomed – just about the worst posture for an injured back. I needed a few months away from the office to rebuild my strength.

Sometimes, I overdid things, and paid the price. Pain shot across my back as nerve endings sparked against each other and muscles went into spasm. At its worst, it felt like an electric storm arcing across my body; convulsions of my vertebrae that made sleep impossible.

I felt stuck. The accident kept replaying in my mind, a form of post-traumatic stress disorder. I woke at night thinking of my children – the youngest only four years old – and how they had nearly lost their dad. I worried that I would be unable to work, that I would become dependent, that I would not be able to provide for my family.

Determined to distract myself from this negative trough of thoughts, I rooted out my birth certificate from its storage place in the pages of a large atlas. For most people, this is the document that confirms their genetic lineage. Adoptees, however, are provided with a shortened version, omitting detail about their birth parents so these cannot be identified.

I never had a birth certificate growing up, but applied for one at the age of seventeen when I needed a passport. As I looked again at it now, I could see that the abridged document given to me then is a remarkable fake. Sure, it bears the official title of 'birth certificate' and gives my correct birth date, but it refers to me by my adopted surname. Worse, and in common with all birth certificates issued to adopted people, it falsely lists Dublin as my place of birth. This, I learned online, is simply because the Adoption Board (now the Adoption Authority of Ireland) is located in Dublin. Under adoption legislation, this document has the legal status of a normal birth certificate, while not providing any information about my genetic parentage.

I took out another document, the certificate of adoption that was provided to Patrick Cullen, 'tradesman', and his wife Mary. My birthplace is given as 'England'.

This I have always known; it is the one reliable fact about my origins that has breached the barrier of secrecy. However, I now saw that more than two years passed before I was placed with my adoptive parents. I was three years old before the arrangement was made permanent.

What on earth caused this delay? These are not just any old two or three years in a life; they are a crucial period in the development of any child. All the research literature points to the importance of the first weeks and months of a baby's life for the formation of bonds with its mother, and with other important adults.

I sought some perspective on this from Dr Tony Bates, one of Ireland's best-known psychologists. I had interviewed Tony years previously about a book he had written on depression, but hadn't seen much of him since. I remember being powerfully affected by the strength of his emotional honesty as he recounted the pain he experienced in his own life. Though I didn't appreciate it at the time, we bonded instantly due to our parallel experiences of childhood separation.

'Developmentally, nothing happens more rapidly and with greater complexity in life than events in the first two years,' Tony told me. 'Everything moves at a rapid rate, with tens of thousands of new brain cells being formed every day.'

Tony kindly devoted an afternoon of his time to exploring my fractured personality at a session in his home under the steep slopes of Ben Bulben in County Sligo. 'You were three when you were formally adopted,' he pointed out. 'You had lived a whole lifetime before then. There seems to have been a lot of upheaval during this time, with you moving from place to place and carer to carer, and you were helpless in the face of it. That is so disruptive for a child.'

In Tony's view, 'what happened then is the wound that shaped so much of what was to follow. You went through a whole lifetime of experiences even before you were adopted'.

If anything, he said, my path through life was determined less by adoption and more by the 'traumatic separation' I experienced in those first years of life. Those years were 'the wound that shaped so much' of what happened later.

And yet these years remained a blank for me. It was time, I decided, to fill them in.

8

In the early 1970s, Marian Grove teemed with young life. Though I lacked brothers and sisters, every other home was packed with gaggles of small boys and girls. The area formed a vast, mutualised childcare zone. We were left free to roam all day; adults appeared only to call us in for dinner. What we did on any given day depended on who showed up on the road. The boys played endless games of football; the girls skipped or pushed toy prams. I felt at home now in the estate. Still, when we joined up for street games – hopscotch, relievio, red rover, rounders – I fretted that I would be the last child picked for a team.

The grounds of the Hallmark card factory at the end of the road were perfect for hide-and-seek, ball games, or just hanging around. We played whatever was to be seen on the telly at the time: football in the winter, tennis during Wimbledon, our version of cricket after that, using the stumps Dad made. Everything had its season – marbles, conkers, robbing apples. Fads disappeared as fast as they arrived.

There were tall trees to climb, outbuildings to hide in and door-knockers to knock before running away. In summer, we used our fathers' magnifying glasses to melt the tar on the road and torture ants. On dark winter evenings, we transferred our hide-and-seek to the aisles of the local supermarket. Every year, we waited for snow that hardly ever came.

The adults griped about the oases of unruly green space, expanses of concrete, broken pavements and treeless parks in their new suburb, but for us the area provided endless opportunities for exploration and adventure.

I arrived home from my first day at school with bloody scratches and a bite-mark on my face. My mother swung into action, marching me up to the house of the young culprit. 'Don't ever go near my boy again,' she yelled at the poor child, who cowered behind his mother's skirt on the doorstep. Henceforth, I would be wrapped in cotton wool, protected fiercely by my mother from the many perils of the world.

I grew up a quiet child, watchful and sometimes wary. Keen to make new friends, I submitted to the stronger wills of other, more confident boys. When a friend demanded that I swear allegiance to his pet guinea-pig, I was content to do his bidding – but crossed my fingers behind my back. I made sure I was in the gang, but never aspired to lead it.

From the start, Mam had aspirations for me. I would live that better life that had eluded her. Ambition and insecurity drove her parenting style. She constantly strived for my advancement. All I wanted was to kick ball with the other kids.

But my eyesight deteriorated, and I was soon seeing the world through thick glasses. I was not destined to become the hero of my dreams: a Cruyff or a Giles, or an Olympic athlete aiming faster, higher, stronger.

Instead, I read books voraciously, though there were few in the house. I counted six in total, four of them manuals on vegetable-growing. Dad's favourite was a bound copy of the *Reader's Digest Complete Do-it-Yourself Manual*; indispensable for any self-respecting 1970s father needing to build a car port or a rabbit hutch.

The other book was written by my father's grand-uncle, a priest who had emigrated to Australia at the start of the twentieth century. Mam, always questing for respectability, reverentially showed off the book written by 'our monsignor' to visitors. No-one had actually read the book, the history of an order of Irish nuns in Tasmania. On his death, my parents were sent a photograph of the stern-faced cleric in his purple cassock. They placed the framed picture on the shelves alongside the plastic bulls and flamenco dancers brought back by neighbours from their Spanish holidays. Over time, it faded in the sunlight. No more was said of our tenuous Aussie connection.

Though Mam was no book-reader, she never stinted on my access to them. Once a week, we took the bus down to the nearest library, in Terenure. In its modest children's section, I chose the two books I was allowed to borrow while she smoked outside, chatting to anyone she could buttonhole. I read whatever was available – children's classics; abridged versions of nineteenth-century adult adventures such as *The Man in the Iron Mask* and *The Three Musketeers*; books of lists; quiz-books; sports annuals. When I had read all there was to read in the children's section, I moved on to the adult library. Mam boasted to neighbours about my reading prowess, but at home she warned me to borrow only 'proper' books. Occasionally, she flicked through my borrowings, judging the book by the cover rather than the content.

When I was eleven, my parents purchased a set of encyclopaedias for me, though they could ill-afford it. The *Encyclopaedia Britannica*, bought on hire purchase, cost £287 (over €3,000 in today's money). Dad built a bookcase to house the thirty precious volumes.

In time, we got bikes to take us farther afield. None had any gears, so we had to traipse up the steep bits of the Dublin hills beyond Ballyboden. Climbing up to the viewing point at Killakee, we lolled about on the grass to get our breath back, gazing at the smoke-covered city beginning to stretch around Dublin Bay below. Then we got back on our bikes and pedalled down the twisting road at breakneck speed, young and free and oblivious to the existence of helmets.

'Hey, heifer!' Slagging was an occupational hazard growing up in the 1970s, but seldom subtle.

'Four-eyes, come out from behind those glasses!'

'Butter-fingers, couldn't catch a ball if it was put in your hands.'

'Fat bastard.' 'Dodgy bastard.' 'Lucky bastard!'

But never, simply, *bastard*. Somehow, I was never called a bastard for being adopted. I am sure many other adoptees were. There may have been strength in numbers. I was not alone; a scattering of adoptees, enough to count on two hands, lived on the road. Even our Protestant neighbours had adopted children. I never felt less than fully accepted.

Still, from early on, I felt different. Initially, this had nothing to do with being adopted.

The other houses in my street were filled with production lines of children, the washing lines in their gardens drooping with the weight of continuous laundry. Their kitchens smelled permanently of overcooked vegetables. There always seemed to be someone in the toilet you needed to use.

My home was different. Here, quiet prevailed, aside from the always-on radio in the kitchen, set at a low volume to RTÉ. A succession of overweight terriers provided company for me. Dad and I made a family of puppets, and I spent long hours talking to them, acting out different lives in the imaginary world I created.

I was not a pampered child, though, indulged by my mother and father. Money was tight everywhere on our road, expectations of children were modest and parenting operated on a long leash. Everything that was available free I got in generous measure: fresh air, time to myself, love, put-downs. Material goods were another matter; they had to be scrimped and saved for. They were doled out sparingly, if at all.

Yet I lacked for little. Football boots, bikes and Lego sets duly arrived on birthdays or at Christmas, but the rest of the year was quiet. As a family, we never went on holidays. Mam said this was because Dad was busy painting houses in the summer. I consoled myself with the knowledge that most of the neighbouring kids got no farther than a caravan site in Wexford. The chipper was a treat each Friday, followed by ice-cream cut from a block and sandwiched in a wafer. There were no restaurant meals.

There was a huge contrast between the quiet of my own home and the fizzing energy I witnessed in larger households. Over in my friends' houses, the ping-pong of sibling rivalry played out before my astonished eyes. Maximum decibels, constant infighting. Was this what *normal* families looked like?

Back in my house, there were library books, toy sets with no parts missing and endless time to play with them. I spent hours leafing through the wafer-thin pages of my encyclopaedia, ingesting facts for the want of anything else to do. I didn't have to worry about someone finishing the corn flakes or the last of the milk before me. At dinner on Sundays, I never had to compete with siblings for the breast of the chicken. I was a rarity of the time, an only child.

I was ten when the weirdness started. The first time it happened, I was reading a story by torchlight under the bed covers. A lion got injured. It died. I burst into tears. But these were no ordinary tears; they flowed and flowed without a let-up. Sobbing uncontrollably, I struggled to breathe. Never before had I experienced such an overpowering sadness.

I drifted off to sleep eventually, but cried again the next night, and the next again. Soon, I was crying several times a day, without warning. The tiniest things set me off. On Christmas Day, while watching *Ben-Hur* with my parents, I welled up suddenly. I ran to the bathroom to save face and recover.

At first, I tried to hide my crying. I had no idea why I was feeling this way. It was terrifying. If an attack came on, I would run out of the room or hole myself up in the toilet until things calmed down. This was not a long-term solution. I felt it must be obvious to others that I was acting strangely. So I told my parents what I was going through. I cannot explain the tears, I said, my eyes already watering; they just happen.

Sharing my secret helped a little. And, to their credit, they did all the right things. They took me to the GP and then to some kind of therapist, a psychologist probably. I saw a succession of adults with glasses and clipboards and lots of questions. These professionals had no answers for me. Wait and see, they told my parents. I was mystified. A black cloud had moved over my world, and it was refusing to budge.

'Is something bothering you?' Mam and Dad constantly asked. 'Is someone getting at you? We won't stand for that, you know that.' They grew convinced there must be some external cause, some identifiable villain to blame.

Sadly, there was nothing or no-one I could point the

finger at. I took the vitamins they gave me, and resisted the desire to stay in my bedroom. The only thing I was certain was bothering me was them constantly asking me what was bothering me. Maybe these things just happened, I told myself.

Life went on. The seasons changed. The arrival of spring brought better days, a sliver of hope. It has always been my favourite time of year. I got out more. I managed not to miss any school, though there were days when I had to run off to the bathroom suddenly when I was feeling overcome.

After many months, the cloud started to lift. The tears flowed less frequently. And then, for no reason at all, one day, they were gone. My brief experience of childhood depression was over.

The episode left me confused. I was, surely, not the only person to have suffered an episode like this, but I had no way of knowing. It wasn't something I dared mention to others. The frightening aspect for me was the lack of an obvious cause. One day everything was dandy; the next day I crashed.

Or perhaps there *was* a cause, one I was unable to recognise. Or one I refused to recognise or acknowledge. Could my experience have stemmed from events in my earlier life, whether I remembered them or not?

9

The dust lies an inch thick on the old cardboard Dairy Box container in the attic. It has been an effort to get here, flashes of pain streaking across my body as I climb gingerly up the access ladder and slither into the tight space under the eaves. Brushing my forearm across the top of the box reveals the cover illustration I remember from my childhood, of three flowers in an oval centrepiece. And the label I wrote years before, just after my mother died. I have found what I am looking for.

I am still on sick leave, with time on my hands. The path to learning more about my origins goes through the Catholic Protection and Rescue Society of Ireland (CPRSI). The agency that organised my adoption and holds all my records has operated behind a wall of secrecy for most of its history, but I am aware that times have changed more recently. There is an air of *glasnost* about these days; the agency claims to be more open to approaches from the likes of me. Yet dealing with the CPRSI will take time, I know from experience. I will have to be both persistent and patient.

Previously, when I looked for information, there were long delays before I even saw anyone. And when I did, staff were clam-like and often unhelpful; despite talk of modernisation, secrecy remained their imperative. Crucially, the law remains stacked in the agency's favour, and against the disclosure of information to adoptees.

Biding my time on this front, it makes sense to start my inquiries, however belatedly, with the story of the adoptive parents who nurtured me.

'Mam/Dad' written in fading blue ink on the lid: the few surviving physical records of my deceased parents, barely enough to fill an old chocolate box.

Prising open the container, I sift through its contents. Black-and-white photos of their wedding in a Dublin church, long before I arrived. A few picture albums with photographs that are mostly out of focus, off-centre or over-exposed. A newspaper supplement published to mark Pope John Paul II's visit to Ireland in 1979. Cufflinks and a narrow tie that Dad once wore to my Confirmation; some earrings that must have belonged to Mam. An early nineteenth-century coin handed down within the family, its surface worn smooth with the hands of so many people, our family's only heirloom. I wanted to learn more about my parents, but it didn't seem there was much to go on.

My parents seldom dwelt on events that occurred before I arrived in their lives. And, like most children, I wasn't that curious about it, so asked little. When they did talk about the past, their memories were often tinged with bitterness. Early on, I learned that Mary and Pat had both suffered setbacks in life, events that scarred them permanently.

Mam once let slip that she had 'lost a baby'. It was one of those times, probably over dinner, when adult concerns barged briefly into my world, only to be supplanted quickly by the usual childhood preoccupations. Still, the phrase lingered with me. It sounded as though this baby had fallen out of her shopping-cart or slipped down between the cushions of the settee.

She didn't elaborate, then or later, other than to complain generally about her treatment by the medical and legal professions. Growing up, I seldom pressed her on the subject, sensing her reluctance to delve into the past. This was a boat I didn't feel I wanted to rock.

Sifting through the box, I recalled the palpable sadness that hung around my mother when she made this disclosure. At the time, I was probably too young to appreciate the impact it had on her, though I was only too aware of its indirect effect on me.

The box was nearly empty now. I found myself regretting that I hadn't held on to more of my parents' keepsakes after their deaths. But we had moved house a few times and space was tight, so some things had to go.

At the bottom of the box, I came across a tightly bound wrap of cloth. In it there was a leather pouch containing a set of envelopes filled with old correspondence and newspaper cuttings. I could not remember seeing this before. Perhaps I had missed it in the upheaval following my mother's death all those years before. Or maybe I did see it, but assumed it was of little interest.

What I read now, piecing together the story told by the scraps of tattered papers before me, astounded me. Here, detailed in the formal language of doctors and judges, was evidence of a trauma endured by my mother that was even more severe and life-changing than the accident I had recently suffered.

10

A young woman strolls back from Mass on a pleasant summer morning. There is no hurry on her, what with it being a Sunday and her head brimming with plans for the baby. She walks alone, since her husband is working today. As a painter and decorator, he has to put in long hours in summer to make up for the inevitable winter slowdown, when bad weather makes outdoor work impossible and he will inevitably be laid off.

Mary loves that no-one knows she is pregnant – apart from Pat, of course. She isn't showing yet, but she will be soon. Family and friends will have to be given the news. So much to organise, too, but proper plans for the baby can be made only after people have been told it is coming.

It is August 1958, and the couple have been married for over a decade. A baby is long awaited. There have been miscarriages but they are never spoken of. Why else would they delay so long in making the announcement? The wait hasn't stopped Mary making plans in her head. It is surely time for Pat to paint the box bedroom for the baby. And to finally take up her cousin Teresa's offer of hand-me-down baby clothes.

She frets about money; everyone does these days, with the state the country is in. For now, Pat is lucky. He has a good job with a building contractor, a large Protestant firm, decent employers. But there is no knowing how long it will last. He has been forced to go to England many times over the years, whenever painting work dries up at home. It is the same story all around: some of the neighbours have been forced to sell up and emigrate, only a few years after buying their house.

Mary's thoughts are interrupted by the sound of an engine, backfiring probably. Funny that – there isn't usually much traffic along this lane, especially at weekends.

The noise intensifies, the whine of a small engine revving. Abruptly, it is joined by the high screech of brakes. Mary feels compelled to look behind her. She sees a motorcycle bumping up the kerb, a malevolent missile heading in her direction. It twists into a long sideways skid, the back wheel now leading the charge towards her. She raises her hands instinctively to protect herself and the baby in her belly. Mechanical and human sounds commingle. A final rev, an anguished wail. Silence.

Mary isn't too badly hurt. According to her doctor, there are 'various injuries of a superficial nature and a considerable degree of shock'. That evening, though, she starts haemorrhaging. This continues for two days until, at thirty-eight, Mary loses the child she had carried for four months.

In the hospital, the doctors pass judgement. 'In my opinion there can be no doubt whatsoever that the accident was the direct cause of her losing the first pregnancy after eleven years [sic] of sterile marriage,' one pronounces. On examination, he declares her pelvic organs 'absolutely normal' with no 'mechanical obstruction' to her becoming pregnant again.

Yet she does not conceive. Another doctor puts this down to 'neurasthenia, due to continued disappointment over the loss of her baby and the inability to dismiss the incident from her mind'.

The dictionary defines neurasthenia as 'a syndrome marked by physical and mental fatigue accompanied by withdrawal and depression'. It began as a disease of overworked factory bosses in the nineteenth century, but soon morphed into a women's disease – invariably diagnosed by male doctors. Mam's doctors are blaming her inability to conceive on her mental state. The problem is in her head.

The couple keep trying, but to no avail.

Searching newspapers archives in the National Library, I come across a short article about my mother, the only time her name appeared in the media. She sued the motorcyclist, who lived locally, for riding 'in a manner dangerous to the public'. The case was sent to court. The legal teams required her to undergo multiple medical examinations.

The motorcyclist's insurance company accepted liability but offered Mam just £250 for her injuries. The loss of an unborn baby did not figure in its calculations.

Two years on from the accident, a settlement was reached

in the High Court. The insurer's penny-pinching was exposed in court. 'Mrs Cullen, who had suffered multiple lacerations of the skin, and abrasions on both legs, is to be paid £1,150 and costs, without admission of liability,' according to the newspaper report of the case. The sum represents about €28,000 in today's money.

A month later, Mary and Pat lodged £900 of this amount in a Northern Bank account. They resumed their efforts to conceive. Mary went from consultant to consultant, the fees eating up her settlement. Despite the doctors' assurances that all was well, she remained unable to bear a child.

For the rest of her life, Mam complained loudly but generally about greedy lawyers and incompetent doctors. In her anger, she left no space to acknowledge the trauma she had suffered through a collision that deprived her of her child, and any ability to conceive again. Closure on this tragedy would elude her.

The medical bills continued to drain their funds. Mary remained alone in their house in the new estate in the suburbs of Dublin during the day while Pat worked. He had decorated all the rooms, working mostly during winter when his painting work dried up. But for what? Just the two of them now in a three-bedroom house with a handsome garden, and no babies to fill it. A great melancholy permeated the house. Pat must have dreaded coming home after work.

Outside, the street swarmed with children. In the neighbouring houses, two families had seven children apiece, two had four and there were three children in each of the remaining houses. The only exception to this fecundity was the bachelor living next door. Mary took to watching activities on the road from behind the net curtain on her landing window, no doubt wishing things had turned out differently.

Relatives suggested a solution – why not adopt a child?

It was the early 1960s, the cusp of an era of enormous social transformation in much of Europe and North America. Not so in Catholic Ireland, where the winds of change turned up as the slightest of breezes. In western Europe's most conservative backwater, it remained illegal to sell or import contraceptives, sex outside marriage was anathema and most women were rendered powerless beyond the confines of the kitchen. Divorce would not be legalised for another thirty years and abortion would remain taboo for half a century.

Adoption, in contrast, had been legal for more than a decade. And while society remained highly traditional, extramarital births were growing year on year. Most of these babies ended up being placed for adoption, due to the enormous stigma attaching to births outside marriage.

Adoption, tightly controlled by Catholic and Protestant agencies, was the favoured strategy for dealing with the surging number of extra-marital births. The adoption deal was regarded as a win-win for all concerned: the single mother was freed of a financial burden and the shame of raising a child outside marriage in a fiercely disapproving society; the adoptive parents got the child they were unable to conceive; and the child was promised a stable roof over their head.

Mary and Pat, now in their forties, knew time was not on their side. A local priest put them in touch with an adoption agency, but there were forms to fill out, documents to submit by post, checks to undergo. More precious time went by.

This was long before the introduction of in vitro fertilisation (IVF) and other fertility treatments. The options for women struggling to conceive were limited. Consequently, the demand for babies to adopt was overwhelming. Irish babies were in huge demand, not just at home but also in the United States. Money changed hands as thousands of babies were exported.

For unknown reasons, Mary and Pat were passed over for several years while others were matched with the babies becoming available for adoption. Their prospects got worse from 1964 when the minimum age for adopting was reduced from thirty years to twenty-five years; now they were competing against much younger couples for the limited number of children available.

The money from the settlement was almost gone. By 1965, there was just one shilling left in the account. They were running out of options.

Mary must have struggled to comprehend this reversal of fortune. There she was, attending Mass every day, while Pat, suited and scrubbed clean, accompanied her to the church on Sunday mornings. They didn't drink, apart from her weekly bottle of Guinness for medicinal purposes. He had stopped smoking – not even a pipe. Was it their age? Their lack of education? Their lack of income?

However, not all babies waiting to be adopted were born equal. Some were in less demand than others. Mixed-race babies, for example. Or babies with medical issues who could not be passed fit for adoption. And even though a baby's medical problems might resolve, by the time this happened he or she could well be too old for adoption.

The woman at the adoption agency told the couple that she had one such baby on her books: a boy who was in foster care. The boy was waiting for the medical all-clear on a heart problem, though she didn't tell Mary this detail. The woman knew the child would have to be placed soon; otherwise it would be too late and he would have to go to a home. His foster care had already cost a lot of money and there would be a further outlay if he moved to a home. Who would foot the bill for that?

So, the woman reasoned, why not place the near aged-out baby with the near aged-out parents?

Mary had her heart set on a girl, but she was pleased with the offer and determined not to lose another child. She vowed to hold this boy as close to her as she possibly could, to shelter and protect him, and to love him as her own.

Which is how, due to an accident that happened long before he was born, a small boy with a slightly wonky heart was sent to live with Mary and Pat Cullen.

11

When I was small, Mam would regale me with stories of her childhood – the lavish gifts she received from her uncle, how she was paraded around town on his horse-drawn carriage, their visits to the Dublin Horse Show. Her uncle, who was childless, was a successful businessman who owned an iron foundry and a scrap metal business, and she was the apple of his eye.

But it was far from finery Mary Doherty started life. Born into a large Dublin family, she lived in a cottage off Clanbrassil Street, in Harold's Cross. Her father was a butcher with a shop on Thomas Street, who lost an eye in an accident with a skewer. All the Doherty men worked hard in the trade, at a time when butchers slaughtered their animals as well as selling the meat. They toiled long hours in freezing abattoirs and store rooms, lost digits to wayward blades and contracted TB, a common disease of the period. Most died in their sixties, though both Mary's parents were long-lived.

While other branches of the family prospered, her father was forced to close his shop because, my cousins tell me, of his over-generosity towards customers. In a custom not unusual in that era, Mam was farmed out to a relative. She went from being another mouth to feed to a golden child, constantly spoiled by her man-about-town uncle and his wife.

Sadly, after a few years with the uncle, he fell ill and died in his prime. Mam was forced to return to her overcrowded family home. From having her own room and a gilded life in her uncle's house, she once again had to share a bed with her sisters. She was left with a sense of there being a better life, though now it was beyond her grasp.

She left school at the age of twelve. There were floors to be swept and clothes to be washed by hand. She helped her grandmother to feed the pigs and chickens, and grew vegetables and flowers out the back of the cottage. She and her brother were keen dancers, and she loved to wear beautiful gowns, which she would lock in the wardrobe, away from her sisters.

Like other women in newly independent Ireland, my mother was doubly condemned to the hardship of life at home and limited prospects outside it. In her case, she had glimpsed a promised land of comfort and freedom, but it had been snatched away. As memories of that earlier taste of a better life with her uncle faded, she was sent out to work until she could be married off.

As for Dad, painting stretched back generations in his family. Born in rural Wicklow just weeks before the Easter Rising of 1916, he moved with the family to Dublin's North Strand as a young child. Despite this switch to the bustle of the big city, the Cullens remained gentle, countrified folk with a relaxed, even dreamy, approach to life.

I have a single class photo from his time at St Canice's Christian Brothers school on the nearby North Circular Road, which he attended up to the age of twelve. As he leaves education, the Irish Free State is trying to find its feet after years of insurrection and civil war. The future is hugely uncertain. The boys, formally kitted out in jackets, ties and short trousers, glare at the camera with a grim ferocity, their tightly folded arms matching the scowls on their faces. Dad, in contrast, looks softer-skinned, his expression neutral, his thoughts elsewhere.

He trained as a house-painter, spending seven years as an apprentice before getting his union card. Work was plentiful at first as the new Irish state built thousands of homes after Dublin's inner-city slums were cleared. But before long, Ireland was mired in a trade war with the United Kingdom. The economy slumped. As war loomed in Europe, Dad emigrated to find work.

Though never settling permanently in England, he racked up enough time there for my mother to qualify, many years later, for a small part-pension from the UK social services. He brought home no mementoes, or memories he was prepared to talk about, aside from a small tattoo. As a child sitting in his lap many years later, I would scratch the blurry blue anchor on his forearm with unceasing curiosity, but he never told me how it came to be etched there.

Returning to Ireland after the war, Dad worked alongside at least three of his brothers on housing projects around Dublin. Whenever work dried up, he took the boat back to England.

Mam and Dad went out with each other for a while but broke up when he emigrated. Six years later, she was walking out with another young man on Grafton Street when Dad caught her eye again. The other beau was quickly dispatched once Dad had asked her out to a dance. Engagement followed quickly; I imagine Mam didn't hang around in sealing the deal. Dad would have gone along with her decision, as he always did.

This was all long before my time, of course, but a few scraps of correspondence survive. From his family home on Dublin's north side, Dad sent a letter, undated, to Mam in her family home on the south side of the city. Impatient yet chaste, the letter shows the extent to which young adults were in thrall to their parents at the time:

Dearest May,
I want to go across to your house Fri night as I would like to see your people about our engagement. Please wait in, I will be over as early as possible. Well darling, I am sorry this is such a dull week for you but it's the same for me.
Yours with all my love xxxxx

The letter, which I came across long after his death, is as close as I ever got to hearing my father on matters of the heart. That, and a brief fragment of another undated letter that has survived on crumpled paper:

> *...well sweetheart I better not tell you too much in this letter or I'll have to send you a blank page for my next as I will be lost for news, so I'll ring off now. Sending you all my love,*
> *Yours, Pat xxxxxx*

They married in August 1948, exchanging a pair of 22-carat rings from McDowell's jewellers on O'Connell Street, popularly known across Dublin as 'the Happy Ring House'. Photos show Dad sporting a dickie-bow and double-breasted suit with wide lapels – looking like a genial mobster – confetti strewn like unseasonal snow about his head and shoulders. Mam is wearing an ankle-length, high-collared dress that covers her arms, together with gloves and a veil, and she holds a bouquet of long-stemmed white carnations.

Their first home was a rented flat in Portobello, near her parents, said to be permanently damp due to its proximity to the Grand Canal.

The 1950s brought stirrings of hope for Ireland and for my parents. New housing estates sprang up around Dublin, oases of promise amid the general gloom of a failing state. Private house-builders fashioned lines of identikit houses out of farms and golf courses, though much-needed shops and schools were often slow to follow. Migration from rural Ireland to Dublin – 'the big smoke' – grew apace.

For the second time in her life, a promising vista opened up for my mother: the prospect of owning her own house and garden. She coveted the space she lacked growing up in the family home – the freedom to close the door and leave the rest of the roiling world behind.

After years of saving, my parents found a house they liked and put up £100 to buy it from the Cooperative Home Building Society, against a purchase price of £1,760 – a modest €56,000 in today's values. The price was discounted in return for Dad painting houses in the estate. Dublin County Council funded the mortgage, with repayments fixed at £7 a month (the equivalent of €240 in modern terms) for forty years – a long-term arrangement unimaginable today.

There was also a yearly ground rent of £12 and 10 shillings, to be paid to the historic landowner. This was an additional burden my parents and their neighbours deeply resented. Whenever they were in financial difficulties, the ground rent went unpaid, prompting a shower of threatening letters from an aggressive solicitor in Merrion Square. Much later, to my amusement, the solicitor popped up as a leading light in a clutch of Catholic conservative organisations run out of his prestige offices in Georgian Dublin.

My parents moved into the Marian estate, not far from Rathfarnham village in south Dublin, in 1956. The Marian Year, designated by the Catholic Church for particular veneration of Mary, mother of Jesus, had taken place two years earlier.

A wavy road lined by cherry trees led down to the

cul-de-sac where their house stood, three-bedded and semi-detached like the others. To the south, overgrown fields stretched out beyond the ragged edge of the built city. Farther in the distance, you could see the low Dublin hills, at least until newer houses were built that blocked the view. To the north lay a farm that later became the US-owned Hallmark greeting card factory, where many of the local women, my mother included, found employment. Eastwards, the backs of our houses abutted older, genteel homes with well-tended rose bushes in fine gardens, from which the pock-pock of tennis balls could be heard in summer.

The times were challenging, but for now my parents were on the up-and-up. They had a stable marriage and a roof over their heads, so long as they could afford the mortgage. Ireland's fortunes had started to improve. Seán Lemass became taoiseach in 1959 with promises to build up the economy and create jobs, even if it meant inviting in foreigners (such as Hallmark) to do this.

Dad set up a painting contracting business with some colleagues. Catching the wave of rising optimism, he was soon employing 'scores' of workers, Mam would later tell me.

My parents' run of good luck didn't last. Mam suffered her accident. Dad's business collapsed in one of Ireland's periodic slumps. His partners ran off, lumping him with substantial debts that took years to pay off. His confidence shot, he went back to working for others and generally keeping his head down in life.

The 1950s wasn't always the wasteland described in subsequent accounts. Ireland was a more tightly knit community then, and people helped each other. However, the documents I retrieved from the attic hint at how hard life was for my parents at the time. They struggled for years to meet the repayments on their mortgage. Dad was forced to travel to England repeatedly for work. Mam even joined him there for a time, leaving empty their cherished new home in Dublin. Surviving bills, including a letter from the council's health department threatening legal action against my mother over a debt of £1 for hospital treatment, give an idea of the pressure they were under.

By the time I arrived, my father was lumbered with a profound lack of self-belief. He was a skilled craftsman, but no business genius. Life events had robbed him of any vestige of confidence. He was, effectively, a shadow of himself – a loving, gentle but broken man. Mam called the shots at home, and he seemed happy with that, even when handing over the manila envelope containing his wages to her every Friday evening.

But at least he had found regular employment again, as a set painter at Ardmore Studios in Bray. The work was well paid but as dull as, well, watching paint dry. But one evening, according to one of my mother's more fondly remembered tales, Dad turned up on his scooter with another man riding pillion. The man was compact and handsome and, bizarrely, his face was blackened with soot.

The strange visitor was the English actor James Mason, who was playing a fighter pilot in the First World War drama

The Blue Max, the film Dad was working on that summer. Mason had been shooting flight scenes for the film over the plains of Kildare earlier in the day. Needing an urgent lift into Dublin after his chauffeur-driven limousine broke down, he somehow ended up on the back of Dad's Lambretta. Once she had recovered from the initial shock, Mam served the film star tea and biscuits in our kitchen while a replacement car arrived to pick him up. 'If only I had had a sliced pan in the house, I could have given him a few sandwiches,' she told me later.

My parents' world was unbelievably circumscribed. Mam talked about 'the country' as though it were a single place on the map, inhabited by a foreign race. Before I turned into a truculent teenager, Dad took me for weekly spins on his scooter. A kind neighbour had constructed a metal seat, which my father strapped onto the back of the scooter before tying me in. Although lashed together with a variety of ropes, the contraption never fell off. Off we rode each Sunday afternoon, roaming the by-ways of the Dublin and Wicklow mountains, skimming stones on the dark waters of corrie lakes and stopping for treats in local villages.

A favoured route followed the coast road south from Dublin, the scooter puttering up the hill from Dalkey towards the Vico Road, with its panoramic views of Dalkey Island and the pebbled beach below, and farther south to Bray Head and the Wicklow mountains. The houses here were enormous.

Dad stopped the scooter on the hilly road above Sorrento Terrace one particularly fine afternoon, and pointed out towards the sea.

'Look at that – the fifth most beautiful bay in the world. Almost as good as Naples.'

Father and son enjoyed a moment of quiet admiration together, hands shielding the sun from our eyes as we scanned the rippling waters for boats. I thought I could see mountains in Wales across the Irish Sea but it was probably just low cloud.

'Let's go to Naples some time, Dad. Let's see if it's as good as this.'

Dad sighed. He knew he wouldn't be going to Naples. He didn't even have a passport.

On another trip, after the scooter had laboured painfully up the steep hill to Lough Bray in County Wicklow, Dad cut the engine suddenly.

'We have to go back now, son.'

'But why, Dad? Let's go on. Up there.'

I pointed in the direction of the mist-covered bog ahead. I hadn't a clue where the road led but I was keen for the adventure to continue.

'I don't know where that goes. It might be dangerous; it's wild up there in the mountains. We'll have to go back.'

There was no persuading him. We turned for home, my dad easing back down the hill with great caution while I worked through a tantrum in my little throne on the back of the scooter.

That here-be-dragons limit to Dad's world was less than 25 kilometres from our home.

12

At home, I relearn walking, bending over, lifting light objects. Cycling and swimming are possible again, but running is out, for now, and maybe for good. Bones mend and wounds heal. The tiny incisions made by the surgeons in my back all but disappear. I begin to feel normal again.

Yet time hangs heavy. At night, I continue to re-enact the fall in my mind, often waking up bemused to find that I am not actually falling through the air. I pass the leaden hours until daylight ruminating on what I have learned since the fall.

The accident has had a profound effect on me, this mental self-reckoning it has triggered, in addition to the physical impact. I had always considered myself self-aware, and yet the mountain showed me how little I understood.

During the days, I grow rueful. I have left it so late to embark on a search for my beginnings. Both my adoptive parents are dead, so I don't have to feel awkward or duplicitous about researching my birth parents. But if I had any questions for Mary and Pat, they are not around to answer them.

At least I have made a start, working from the scant artefacts of their life. Uncovering the details of Mam's pregnancy loss and her subsequent infertility has helped me make more sense of my upbringing. Overall, my parents gave me a happy start in life as an adopted child, though there were bumps along the way. I was housed, fed and shod, and grew up healthy and active. I received more love than any child could possibly have expected, the experience intensified by my late arrival and the fact that I ended up as my parents' only child. And yet things happened that should not have happened. That for so long I preferred not to acknowledge. That now weigh on me hugely.

It is the early 1970s and I am in the darkened front room of the house. There are net curtains on the window, hanging drapes to either side and a wooden, hand-painted pelmet above it. All conspire to make the room gloomy.

Outside, the day is bright and sunny. The pink and white cherry trees on the road are in blossom. It is spring, the school year is nearing its end and the long, lazy days of summer are approaching. In the distance, I hear random shouts, the sounds of other children playing some game or other. I should be out on the road, kicking a ball or trying to melt the tar with my magnifying glass. But I cannot join them. I stay hunkered under the table. I have done wrong.

I try to breathe as softly as I can, though my chest is heaving and my pulse is racing.

The overhang of the tablecloth billows gently upwards as the door jerks open. Someone has entered the room, dressed in nylon pants and nylon socks, moving quickly with small steps. They are wearing just one slipper.

A slapping sound breaks the quiet. The second slipper is being slapped first against the table, then against their hand.

'Come out, ye bowsie.'

I hold my breath, my cheeks reddening, tears brimming in my eyes.

I have done wrong; I just do not know what it is.

'Ye little cur. You're only a proper tike.'

The nylon pants are ranging around the room now. She doesn't know yet that I am here.

'Ye dirty fecker.'

The glassware on the table jumps and clinks as the slipper is brought down sharply on its surface once more.

'You're not fit to be here. I shoulda never have taken ye in. I shoulda left ye with your fancy one.'

The voice is shouting now. Growling almost, with the effort. There is grief in it as well as anger, but the grief won't hurt me.

'But she wouldn't have ye, would she?'

Tears now, the voice faltering.

'She didn't want you. Dumped you so she could go off hooering around the place.'

The penny drops. Of course she knows I am here, knows I am listening. Isn't this where I aways hide?

My chest heaves. I sniff softly.

'Sorry, Mam.' The first words a dam-burst of emotion, my tears following.

I know the warning signals well by now; I can feel the approach of trouble. My heart pulsing wildly and the bile rising in my throat as her red mist descends on the house. Maybe, I think, I can outlast the rage. Maybe the worst of her anger will pass before she can lay a hand on me.

So I stay hiding, dumbly, under the stupid table.

No escape this time. The yellow checked cloth is flicked back with one clean movement. Somehow the delph on the table survives. I look up at her face, spittle-flecked and swollen with anger. My mother is barely recognisable to me.

A throaty roar from within her. She reaches in with a surprisingly strong arm, grabs me by the cow's lick on my forehead, pulls me towards her. She has never let me grow my hair long so there isn't much to grasp. My head jerks back as the chestnut strands slip out of her hold.

I crouch farther back into the shadow of the table-top. The slippered foot arcs blindly under the table but doesn't come close to kicking me.

'Get out of there, ye filthy kinatt.'

Now she has hold of my ear and she is pulling me out of my hiding place. I let out a cry. It's not the physical pain. More tears flow.

Can you roar out of sadness, out of dreary familiarity with a piece of cruel theatre being acted out yet again? Whatever – I do nothing to resist. It hurts less that way.

What have I done? What will I say? What can I say when I don't know what I have done?

But it doesn't matter because there are no words. I am being punched in the sides now, but Mam is tiny, her punches no more than feathery prods in my abdomen.

Not hurting at all, yet still hurting.

In time, I promise myself, I will grow tall, and learn how to grab hold of my mother's whirling arms. One day, I will pin those arms back to her sides, and leave the room in disgust.

Today, though, I am small, vulnerable and exposed. All I can do is cry.

And all *she* can do now is cry, and keep slugging me with her arms. They are moving more slowly now, the punches are dissolving into a clinch, a hug. Now she is gripping me tight with both fists, her head sunk in my chest. Her shouts have become mumbles of remorse.

'I'm sorry. I'm so sorry, son. I don't mean it. I never mean it, you know that. It's only because I love you.'

'I'm sorry too, Mam.'

But what am I sorry for? I can breathe again now, and sob, and even hug her back, because I know the worst has passed and things will return to normal.

Until the next time.

Mam's mood swings lasted years, and grew worse as I got older. I never understood them as they occurred. I wasn't a perfect son, but I seldom did much to provoke these outbursts. Now at least, having researched the detail of her accident, I better appreciate why my mother – this woman whom I ended up with through the lottery wheel of adoption – carried such anger. But part of me will forever be that small boy under the table.

Though my adoption was designed to fill the void caused by the loss of her baby, Mam never got over that earlier tragedy. The accident occurred years before I arrived in her life, but it was to cast a long shadow on the time we spent together.

It wasn't just the trauma of being hit by a motorcycle and losing a baby a few days later. My parents experienced the subsequent court case as a scarring event in itself. Mam wasn't prepared for the level of intrusive questioning she had to undergo in order to vindicate her rights, and the grind of trying to conceive again. She won her case in court, but there was really no making up for her loss.

Reading the newspaper cuttings and remembering Mam's discomfort about ever talking about the accident, it is clear how deeply shaken she was after her life was turned upside down. The settlement negotiated related to her injuries alone, with no account taken of the demise of her child. Society was less sensitive then to baby deaths, including miscarriages and stillbirths.

Unfairly perhaps, I came to doubt her stories about botched operations and crooked lawyers. My mother could be a fabulist; she told fibs easily and regularly if they made the world accord more to the way she wanted it to be. Even as a child, I learned to spot the holes in her stories. Yet the documents I found in the attic after her death proved she had endured a terrible trauma.

The accident left her with empty bedrooms in her dream suburban home. There were sandwiches to make and flasks to fill for Dad each day before he left for work, and dinners to put down on the table each evening, but the hours in between must have stretched long and lonely for her. Outside, the children played endlessly, as children do – a constant reminder of her barren status.

Infertility is hard. I imagine it was much harder for a woman back then, in an era when society deemed childbearing and rearing her principal function in life and when alternative life opportunities such as work were so limited.

My parents' attempts to start a family dragged on for many years without success. As a result, their application to adopt began late and took time; Mam was forty-six and Dad fifty by the time I turned up in their home aged two years and four months, a walking, talking toddler.

Back then, it was almost unheard of for a woman to have a child so late. Children born to older mothers were often told crudely they were the 'scrapings of the sack'.

Today, my parents would be considered far too old for adopting a child. Even at the time, they were too old. The officially quoted upper age threshold applied by the adoption agency was forty-five years for a father, and forty-two for a mother.

But at this time, I was also growing too old to be adopted. And I had been diagnosed with a medical issue. A life in foster care loomed for me unless I was placed with a family. Someone somewhere made the practical decision to put the three of us together. So who were these people that brought us together, effectively playing God by creating a family to their own design?

13

The brief advertisement ran in the classifieds of the *Evening Herald* in November 1963: 'We have a few baby boys very suitable for adoption whom we are anxious to place before Christmas. Any kind Catholic family willing to give a baby a home should write to Monsignor (Cecil) Barrett, Catholic Protection and Rescue Society, 30 South Anne Street, Dublin 2.'

Although I was on the books of the Catholic Protection and Rescue Society of Ireland at this time, I can't say with any certainty that the baby boys referred to in the advertisement included me. For some reason, I was to remain in the overall care of the agency for years before I was placed with a family. I certainly wasn't going anywhere that Christmas.

Adoption was big business in the 1960s, and largely controlled by private organisations with religious affiliations. There were dozens of Catholic adoption agencies, along with a few run by Protestant interests. There was even a Jewish agency for adoption and fostering.

Many of these organisations were small, but the CPRSI was in a different league. It was one of the oldest adoption agencies in the state, and for many years the largest. Its pre-eminence was recognised in the 1970s when it became the first adoption agency to obtain state funding.

Founded as a lay organisation in 1913 to combat proselytism, its original mission was to ensure that the babies of Catholic single mothers were not adopted by Protestants. 'It was set up to "save" the souls of Catholics rather than as a child welfare agency,' Colleen Stewart remarked in her PhD thesis on adoption infrastructure in 2013.

From the 1920s, it organised informal placements of children with Catholic families which were called 'adoptions' but which conferred no legal rights on the children or their foster parents. The makeshift nature of adoption in those decades cried out for urgently required reform. Yet the agency originally opposed legal adoption because of the fear that the children of Catholic women would end up in Protestant families. If adoption legislation passed, 'these children will be lost to the Catholic religion forever as once they are legally adopted the person who adopts them can do what he likes with them', it claimed in 1939. After the Second World War, however, the agency switched to supporting adoption as preferable – and cheaper – than long-term institutional care.

Ultimately, legal adoption was introduced in 1953, after the state agreed to the Catholic Church's demand that applicants had to be of the same religion as the child being adopted. The new Irish Republic was slow in introducing this reform; England and Wales had long before passed adoption legislation, in 1926, with Northern Ireland following in 1929 and Scotland in 1930.

The CPRSI was the first agency to apply for registration after adoption was legalised, with the stated object of caring for 'the spiritual and temporal welfare of Catholic unmarried mothers and illegitimate and unwanted children'. By the 1950s and 1960s, when adoption peaked in popularity, the agency was responsible for about one quarter of legal placements in the state. Over the course of a century it created 10,500 files on children who were placed with adoptive parents.

From 1921 until it shut its doors in 2019, the agency operated from a discreet red-brick building off Grafton Street, Dublin's most upmarket shopping area – the address on South Anne Street listed in the newspaper advertisement. I passed through this building multiple times as a tiny child but years would go by before I came to understand its significance in my life.

The penny dropped as a young adult when I was on a night out in Dublin. Tumbling out of Kehoe's pub on South Anne Street at closing time, I came up against a sight that stopped me in my tracks. There, across the road, was the building where my adoption had taken place many years before. I knew this because of the CPRSI brass plate on its front door, which at that moment was being urinated upon by a passing drunk.

Secrecy was the hallmark of the agency's approach to adoption for most of its history. 'Once a baby was placed and the adoption order granted, the agency closed the file in the belief that a birth mother, having made her decision, was free to continue with her life and the adoptive family no longer required input from the agency,' social worker Julie Kerins explained in a book published by the adoption agency in 2013, *All Born Under The One Blue Sky*. Only much later, she added, was this approach tempered by an acknowledgement that 'important issues' could arise after an adoption had been made, and a realisation that adoption was a lifelong process, rather than a once-off transaction. But I was long adopted by then.

While there were dozens of adoption agencies in Ireland, the CPRSI was one of a small number that specialised in repatriating women who had travelled to England to give birth, along with their babies. On their return to Ireland, the women invariably gave up their babies for adoption, either immediately or after a stay in a mother and baby home. The British authorities were only too happy to support this system, in order to minimise the costs they incurred from this flow of pregnant young women across the Irish Sea. Though I was ignorant of the details, I seemed to have been one of the babies caught up in this system.

14

Mam and Dad must have known they were in the last-chance saloon when the opportunity arose to adopt me. They remained nervous even after I was adopted successfully. Throughout my growing-up years, they feared that I would be snatched from them at a moment's notice. This wasn't legally possible, but logic didn't figure in their concerns.

Conscious of their own lack of education, and ignorant of their legal rights, my parents showed extreme deference to the professionals whose paths they occasionally crossed. Mam, in particular, engaged in extravagant forelock-tugging. On encountering someone whom she considered her better, she would adopt a forced hoity-toity accent, littering her speech with malapropisms. The traffic was always 'chopper-block', the hot weather very 'hummus' and an exotic person was apparently 'erotic'. All this delivered in a nasal twang she considered posh.

She wasn't being herself, but perhaps this went back to the protracted process my parents had endured before adopting a child. On several occasions, they were close to adopting a baby but for one reason or another things fell through. They began to suspect their failure to get from one gate to the next was to do with their shortcomings, notably their working-class backgrounds. And all the time they were getting older, and risked being told they were no longer suitable to adopt a child.

There were countless forms to fill out, references to collect and interviews to attend. Assessors visited their home, silently forming judgement on their character and relationship. The process was arduous – as it should be – but they were being assessed as much for being good Catholics as for their potential parenting skills.

Burnt by the experience, my parents never wanted to talk about it, so I have to rely on the accounts of others. Caitríona Palmer, in her memoir of adoption *An Affair with My Mother*, tells how her adoptive parents were repeatedly visited at home by the nun brokering her adoption.

'When they came to visit the house, they went through everything, every single corner of our house. They went from room to room, looking through wardrobes and everything,' Palmer wrote.

The checks continued after she had been placed for adoption. They checked garda records, her mother told her. 'They went to the doctor. They went to … our parish priest at the time. You had to give all your details: who you are, what you had, what your background was, your parents, where you worked.'

Social engineering was built into the process, as were notions of class. Babies from impoverished backgrounds were placed with families of modest means, while the babies born to more middle-class girls were matched with families higher up the social scale. Social workers from my adoption agency endeavoured to place a child 'in an environment slightly better than his natural background', an Adoption Board official concluded in 1956 after a cursory inspection of the CPRSI. A clear majority of placements were made to families from a professional, commercial and technical background, figures show. As late as 1985, the agency was opposed to placing children with couples where the mother was working outside the home, though it made an exception for teachers and, later, doctors.

In one respect, my parents were lucky. The mid-1960s marked the high point of adoption in Ireland, with a glut of available babies, almost all of them born out of wedlock. Before this point, there were fewer babies available, and by the start of the following decade, abortion was available in England as an alternative to adoption, and mothers started keeping their own children in greater numbers.

The best description of the treatment of unmarried pregnant women in Ireland historically comes not from an academic or journalist but from a priest who personally placed hundreds of their children for adoption. To be pregnant outside marriage in early twentieth-century Ireland was regarded as 'a dreadful crime', according to Father James Good, and the women involved were treated as 'outcasts'. 'It was frightening the way unmarried girls were treated. They were banished, straight. The day they found they were pregnant, they headed for England.'

Father Good, an outspoken priest and theologian, who was eventually sent to work in Kenya, was secretary of St Anne's Adoption Society in Cork, established in 1954 with the purpose of arranging the adoption of babies born to Irish unmarried mothers in Britain.

Up to the 1920s, a girl who was pregnant outside marriage was generally 'locked up in a county home for life', he explained in a 2005 interview. In 1922, though, 'state and church got together and decided that girls who had their first baby were regarded as innocent and should be segregated, so they brought in sisters to run (mother and baby) homes in Bessborough, Roscrea and Castlepollard. The idea was that they should be locked up for rehabilitation for two and a half years'.

The requirement to spend such a lengthy period in a mother and baby home made it unattractive to women who had given birth outside marriage. Many left Ireland to escape the stigma attaching to their condition. As a result, Good claims, up to 10,000 Irish women giving birth outside marriage were 'dumped' on Catholic dioceses in England and 'thousands' of their babies were sold as part of informal adoption and boarding out arrangements.

The situation cried out for reform.

Legal adoption was finally introduced in the 1950s, in part due to the concerns over the trafficking of babies from Ireland to childless couples in the US and other countries in the aftermath of the Second World War, and high death rates in some mother and baby homes. The new process provided for the formalisation of adoption through 'adoption orders' approved by the Adoption Board.

The informed consent of the mother or guardian was required and the child had to be aged between six months and seven years before consent could be given (the lower age limit was later reduced to six weeks and the upper limit was increased to eighteen years). Only illegitimate children or orphans could be adopted.

While the aim was to give the adopted child a better life, this was defined in material terms – adopters had to have 'sufficient means to support the child'. Little thought was given to the impact of separating children from their birth mothers.

The legislation, which was introduced after line-by-line vetting by Catholic Archbishop of Dublin John Charles McQuaid, set great store by secrecy. Adoption files were kept sealed for life. Natural mothers had no legal right to information, not even to know whether their child was dead or alive.

Yet the international trade in Irish babies went on. It has been estimated that between 1949 and 1973 more than 2,000 children were sent to America without the knowledge or genuine permission of their mothers. 'While it is true many of the children were afforded a quality of life in America that would never have been available at home, the fact that so many grew to adulthood under assumed names created serious issues of confused identity when the truth was revealed or found out, as did the fact that the real mother's name was in some cases deleted from the record,' according to historian Diarmaid Ferriter.

'It was not an issue of child abuse (in the sense that the Catholic charities by and large did a good job and children were well matched with families), as experienced by many in institutions, but rather the exploitation of mothers,' Ferriter wrote more generally of adoption in *The Transformation of Ireland 1900–2000*.

Illegal adoptions in Ireland, based on the false registration of children as the biological offspring of adoptive parents, also continued. 'Huge sums of money were paid for babies across Dublin where there was a thriving black market from the 1940s into the late 1960s,' adoptee Paul Jude Redmond wrote in his 2018 book *The Adoption Machine*.

None of these disturbing practices were spoken of in the public realm, where the verdict on adoption was invariably positive. 'There is no doubt that the home with an adopted child is always a happy home,' Monsignor Cecil Barrett, director of the CPRSI and the foremost Catholic authority on adoption, boasted in February 1964. At this point, I was under the care of his agency.

Barrett, described by Father Good as McQuaid's 'henchman', espoused secret, closed adoption, where the mother and her child were separated and could never see each other again. The unmarried mother had sinned and her fall was 'too often condoned and excused' by non-Catholic social workers with their 'purely humanitarian' efforts, he explained in his pamphlet *Adoption: The Parent, the Child, the Home*, published in 1952.

'Her condition is referred to as the unfortunate consequences of a slip or a mistake on her part. She has been the victim of bad luck resulting in an unhappy embarrassment and she is advised to be more careful the next time! No cognisance is taken of the gravity of sin or the beauty of the virtue of purity. The very idea of sin would sometimes appear to be outside the ambit of their ministrations.'

Catholic social workers, as Barrett saw it, must concern themselves with the 'moral problems' of the unmarried mother, as well as her social and economic 'difficulties'. 'Mere material assistance may be of no avail, unless the rents in the mother's spiritual fabric have been repaired.'

Barrett, to be fair, pushed for greater professionalism in adoption. It was a risk, he argued, both for the child and the adopters, and should be left to those who were qualified and experienced in this work – by which he meant Catholic adoption agencies. The basis of all good adoption work, he told a meeting of the Dublin Institute of Catholic Theology, was the selection of a particular child for a particular home. This required careful inquiry into the background and medical history of the child, to ensure his or her suitability for adoption.

Yet such was the flow of babies requiring placement at this time that the CPRSI advertised regularly in the newspapers seeking parents willing to adopt. These advertisements tended to feature 'difficult cases' – older or mixed-race children who were harder to place.

'We are very anxious to find a Catholic adoptive home for a lovely baby girl, of mixed race, slightly coloured, aged 7 months,' ran one advertisement in the *Evening Herald*. Another sought to place a 'lovely' baby girl, 'of mixed race but not coloured'.

In my case, for reasons I did not yet understand, my adoption was delayed for years. Boys were always harder to place; the biggest demand from adoptive parents was for girls aged under three months. Finally, in 1965, the adoption agency got on with matching me with a family before it was too late. At this point, I was already two years old. Whatever previous reservations it might have had about Mary and Pat – their precarious financial position, for example – were dispensed with.

I had no idea where I was before my adoption, but I knew the CPRSI used foster homes scattered across Dublin and in north County Wicklow while children were awaiting placement or a decision on adoption by their foster mother. Staff from the adoption agency visited the foster homes every six weeks or so.

I gleaned this information from *All Born Under the One Blue Sky*, the book published by the agency in 2013, containing contributions by former staff, adoptive parents and others 'touched' by adoption.

'The foster mothers were marvellous women, all with families of their own, who provided maternal love and stability for each baby in those early formative weeks or months,' social worker Anne Ronayne wrote in her contribution to the book. 'The foster families were always sad when a child was removed but they accepted that their role was temporary and the baby's future life was with his mother or with adoptive parents.'

The foster mothers received a subsistence allowance. In 1956 this amounted to three pounds and 10 shillings a month per child (about €75 in today's money).

Ronayne recalled driving to foster homes – 'many in the shadow of the Sugar Loaf [a mountain in County Wicklow]'. In these rural homes, the scenery was 'glorious', she cooed, and the pace of life was much slower than in the capital. 'The Dublin homes were different – the pace of life certainly so – but there was genuine goodwill and concern for the babies in all the foster homes.'

I wondered whether this description fitted the environment I found myself in during my first years of life. These were private operators contracted to care for children by a voluntary organisation. There is no record of these homes being inspected, so it is not possible to say what conditions were like in them.

Ronayne's contribution in the book sought to situate the agency's work in the context of the societal mores that prevailed at this time. An important component was repatriation from England: 'The young pregnant woman of that time saw the solution of her problem as flight to England, to avoid the real or perceived wrath of her parents and community. The idea of confiding in parents was rarely considered.'

Irish girls who were in England agreed to the offer of help from her agency 'on our promise of complete confidentiality and an assurance that their "secret" would not be divulged'. She continued, 'This was an absolute condition of their return and completely adhered to by the Society. In the light of today's attitudes this might seem extraordinary or even deceitful but times were different – a fact, not an excuse.'

As to why the girls were encouraged to return, she said English adoption agencies were not equipped to cater for the influx of young pregnant women arriving from Ireland. 'The promise of adoption was guaranteed by us, if this was the mother's wish, but in the mid-20th century there was little other alternative.'

15

I nap in the middle of the day, but I'm more and more active otherwise. I throw myself into housework and small DIY tasks to pass the time, and to distract myself from thoughts welling up inside me, as I ruminate on my past. Yes, I had a happy childhood, as I have been telling people for years. And yet, prompted perhaps by my session of hypnotherapy, my mind keeps dredging up episodes from the past that seem to contradict this.

As I grew up, Mam had more and more bad days. While Dad was out at work, she would take to the bed after lunch, but her mood was little improved afterwards. There was paranoia about neighbours, negative commentary on the state of the world and the usual parental chastisement over the tidiness of my room or my clothes. But what I most remember now was her negative outlook on women. All women, aside from the Blessed Virgin Mary. No girl was good enough for her boy. The entire female gender was a threat to her role as the number one woman in my life.

Somewhere along the way, my mother had ingested a nasty strain of Catholicism that saw every woman, from Eve on, as the cause of Man's downfall in the world. 'Brazen hussies' existed only to bring good men down, she told me many times. Sex – though the word was never used – was their modus operandi.

Was she that unusual? Women were often women's greatest critics in her era. Writing of children fathered out of wedlock, journalist Mike Milotte says in his book on illegal adoptions that 'by and large the attitude was that it was the "fallen" woman who tempted the hapless man into a sinful relationship, men were just men and women had to control the male's "natural urges" by acting modestly'.

In pursuit of peace at home, I spent my teenage years reining in these natural urges. I self-censored. At home, I avoided talking about the opposite sex, for fear of provoking Mam's negative commentary. Both of us acted as though girls didn't exist.

Mam's taunts had made me insecure about my adoption. Dad, anxious to avoid conflict, removed himself from the pitch. I couldn't see farther than trying to keep the peace by dampening my mother's mood swings.

One evening I was sitting in the front room when a shadowy figure appeared in the driveway. Something was pushed through the letterbox, the flap snapping back with a hearty clang. Darting out to the hall, I picked up the pink envelope that lay on the floor and scuttled back to my studies.

'What was that?' My mother had heard the noise from the kitchen.

'Ah, nothing.'

'Nothing? Funny that. I could have sworn I heard something.'

She came into the front room and looked me up and down. The colour rose in my cheeks.

'No. Must have been a noise outside.'

'A noise, is it? Didn't sound like that to me.' Mam left the room with a shake of her head, while wiping her hands on a tea towel.

After a safe interval, I pulled the envelope out of my back pocket. It was addressed to me in large, child-like writing. I had just received my first Valentine's card. Instead of pleasure, all I could feel was terror that it might be found by my mother.

Then there was the time I went with friends to a disco in one of the local tennis clubs. Being a typical self-conscious teenager, I left my glasses at home – never mind that I couldn't see a thing. The dancefloor was a fug, packed out and sweaty. Gauchely, we jigged about to our favourite, 'Echo Beach' by Martha and the Muffins, then wielded our air guitars for Lynyrd Skynyrd's 'Free Bird'. Playing silly was such a release.

I took a breather for the slow set, leaning against a column and squinting about me. My hand accidentally brushed the hand of someone who was resting against the other side of the column. It belonged to a girl my own age. She was just as short-sighted as I was, and had also left her glasses at home.

Myopia is as good an ice-breaker as any. We talked and danced and eventually snogged a bit. At least we could see each other properly at close quarters. Chatting to her friends, I sensed an ease about them that was so different from my world of teenage angst. We arranged to meet at her house the following Sunday.

The week passed with growing excitement about my forthcoming date, but also a dread that my mother would find out and quiz me about it. When Sunday rolled around, I concocted a story about going for a long walk. Leaving home, I tried to appear as casual as possible, wearing nothing out of the ordinary that might raise her suspicion.

There was one problem. My date lived a few miles away; the route I had to take to reach her house was the same one my parents were likely to use on their way to visit a sick relative in hospital.

I took elaborate detours to ensure they would not see me. Approaching the final stretch to her house, there was no option but to walk along the same road they were likely to take. So I jogged from one house entrance to the next, hiding behind pillars and looking back regularly in case my dad's car hove into view.

It was absurd behaviour, but I knew Mam would feel threatened by the presence of another woman in my life. To tell her about my new friend was to risk opening up a Pandora's box of insecurities and accusations. God only knows what she would have said to the poor girl.

I met my girlfriend of a few days for our planned walk but my heart wasn't in it, my mind full of worries. What if my parents passed by? Might there be a public confrontation? Was it worth the effort?

Although I liked her, I didn't make contact again.

Home became a war zone in my teenage years. I was forced in two directions: outwards, towards the embrace of friends; and inwards, into an internal dream world, where I yearned for escape and the chance to bathe in melancholy.

Mam became more, not less, protective as I got older. The world was full of people who would lead me astray. Friends would let me down. Girls were waiting to ensnare me by getting pregnant.

Even inanimate objects aroused her suspicions. Calculators made you forget sums. Books could drive you crazy. Schools and colleges were full of seditious ideas.

Most of this over-mothering was easy to ignore, if a little suffocating. Mary had prime Irish mammy syndrome.

'Mind yourself in town. They'd take the eyes out of your head.'

'Don't go out after that bath, you'll get your end [catch your death] of cold.'

When she hit a bad patch, though, things took a nastier turn. I would wake up early on a Saturday morning to hear the vacuum being bashed loudly around the room directly below me.

I would find her, stiff with rage, holding the vacuum as one might a weapon. 'What time do you call this? Get out there and cut the grass/sweep the leaves/wash the dishes.'

I responded to this unpredictability by dropping the head, following orders and retreating into myself. My world was small but the world of books had no limits. There, I could dream.

Turning inward, I became a serial hobbyist. I collected brightly coloured stamps from across the world, and coins worn down by the years. Without ever leaving my bedroom, I 'travelled' the world on flights of imagination, listening obsessively to shortwave radio stations. I became a prolific writer of letters to embassies and travel agents, requesting brochures on places I could only dream of visiting. At night, I lay in bed wondering how different life might be if I hadn't been adopted, then chastising myself for such heresy.

Desperate for financial independence, I looked for a part-time job. Bar work was one of the few openings for teenage boys keen to earn money. Some friends had been taken on by a local music venue, which agreed to give me a try-out.

I ran the news past my parents, thinking they would be glad I was about to earn money. They didn't say much, which was odd, but I took their silence as approval. I knew there was some alcoholism in the family, which bothered them, but this was true of just about every family I knew.

The next evening, I slipped out of the house quietly for my

first shift, wearing regulation black slacks and a white shirt under my duffle coat. Only on the walk down to the venue did I don the required bow-tie.

My nervousness showed when I made an error on my first order by giving a customer too much change. My float was nearly gone and I had only just started. But the clientele were out for a Friday night and determined to have a good time. Before long, my pockets were bulging with tips.

It was past midnight when I arrived home, tired but satisfied. My clothes smelled of cigarette smoke and my eyes burned. Putting the key in the door, I immediately sensed trouble. Normally at this time, the flickering Sacred Heart lamp under the picture of Jesus cast a lonely red glow on a darkened hall, but tonight the lights were on full. My parents should have been in bed hours ago.

I stepped into the hall as lightly as I could. There was a moment of silence, then Mam rushed out from the sitting room. Dad padded along behind.

'Where have you been? What time do you call this to come home?'

Her eyes had a wild look; her hair was tousled from running her hands through it.

'I was at work. Like I told you.' I took off my coat, placed it carefully on the banister and turned towards my parents, my head bowed, conscious I reeked of other people's stale beer.

'At work? Is that what you call it? Down in the pub with the alcos, the good-for-nothings? You call that work? No son of mine is going to mix with that trash.' Mam was holding a tea towel, which she gave a demonstrative flick.

I found my voice. 'It's a job, Mam. I need to earn money. I told you I was doing this. All my friends are working there.'

'Your friends? Some friends – they'll pull you down into the gutter with them and then leave you to rot. And then what? But maybe you belong there. Maybe that's where you're from.'

Dad, as ever, intervened feebly.

'Son, it's just that—'

Mam was having none of it. Grabbing my jacket, she pulled me with unexpected force into the sitting room, where the lights dazzled my tired eyes.

'It's just that we'd be worried, see, we'd be worried you might get a liking for the drink.' Dad was still in the hall, probably looking uselessly at the floor.

I was angry now too, and weary. Past caring. 'Just because you work in a pub doesn't mean you're going to become an alcoholic.'

That riled her.

'And then coming home with your backchat! Don't you talk to your father like that. Your father, who has scraped and saved for you all his life.' Her voice now a scream, flecks of saliva flying across the space between us.

'Ah May,' Dad said, finally in the room, 'the boy doesn't understand. He's only young.'

'Understand? I'll show him how to understand.'

My mother bowed her head, charged at me, thumped me on each side, reached into my pockets.

'Well, look at this,' she rasped, pulling out fistfuls of coins, my tips for the evening. 'The little millionaire.'

Mam flung the money venomously across the room, the silver glinting briefly under the lights. She grabbed two more fistfuls from my pockets, and scattered those too. A volley of coins smashed against the table lamp, still in its wrapper from the shop. It toppled over and broke. The bulb popped. The three of us froze, suddenly conscious of this moment of idiocy.

I thought about answering back. I thought about telling my mother I was able to make my own decisions. I thought about telling them how silly it was to equate pub work with alcoholism. I thought about defending my friends, whose only crime was to help me find work.

Most of all, I thought about leaving. I could walk out of the room right now. I could go up to my bedroom and barricade myself inside until the morning. Better, I could walk out the front door, and leave this misery behind.

But I had nowhere to go. Who would have me? This was the only family I knew, after I was abandoned by another one. I didn't have anything to my name, except the coins scattered on the floor around me. And what would Mam do? Wasn't this her way of telling me how much she loved me, how she cared for me more than anyone else? Especially more than my other mother.

I backed out of the room quietly, already formulating a plan. First step: get to the safety of bed. Second: try to get things back on an even keel. Third: get out of here as soon as I am old enough.

The coins were still on the carpet the next morning. None of us mentioned the night before, not even to suggest picking them up. Finally, I collected my ill-fated tips in a bowl, which I brought to my room.

I got to keep the money but my career as a lounge boy was over.

16

The day Ireland had been waiting for had finally come. It was 29 September 1979, and Pope John Paul II had touched down in Dublin. One-third of the country was waiting for him in the Phoenix Park for an open-air Mass. I, meanwhile, was starting my career as a rebel.

I raised the garage door as quietly as I could and pushed out Dad's Morris Minor Traveller, with the engine off. Using a combination of hand- and foot-brake, I inched the car down the driveway, taking care not to scratch it on the gate. Turning the steering wheel through the driver window, I managed to align the car straight on the road outside. Now I had to figure out how to make it go.

That wasn't too difficult because Dad had let me sit in the driver's seat a few times. But I'd never properly driven a car – until now. I turned on the ignition; it started first time. Off I went on my illegal self-driving lesson. The roads were empty. More than one million people, Mam and Dad included, were attending the pope's Mass. I had been given a pass because I was due to travel with my school to the youth Mass in Galway the following day.

I drove all over the Dublin mountains, meeting no-one. But when I returned to our estate there was a man standing by the side of the road – Mr Murphy, the only garda in our area. It was too late to avoid passing him, so I drove slowly past his imposing figure, my head bowed and my heart in my mouth. Please don't let me be caught, John Paul, I prayed, and I will *never* do this again. I cut the engine in the driveway and pushed the car the rest of the way into the garage.

I had tired of playing the 'good' adoptee, increasingly feeling suffocated at home. But, in truth, I was too timid to ever become a proper troublemaker. Instead, I became a high-achieving student, earning good grades in exams, winning prizes and captaining the school's quiz team. In doing so, I was both realising Mam's ambitions for me and leaving her world behind.

In class, I developed an argumentative streak, getting kicked out of Religion for questioning the existence of God and having a textbook thrown at me by a frustrated French teacher. I ducked it successfully, the missile making a permanent dent in the wall that someone circled, with my name written alongside.

I came of age just as pop music was going through a period of frantic change. Hard rock and disco were ceding place to punk and new wave. Anger and anarchy replaced the end-phase smugness of the hippy era. A new generation of young people was ripping up the script of popular culture.

It was incredibly exciting to be living through such tumult. The problem was that it was happening elsewhere. The world was changing but mine was not. Others were gelling their hair and slashing their jeans, but I never dared to affect even mild punk airs. I was too bookish and mild-mannered, and far too afraid of my mother's wrath. Mine was a revolution in the head, a love affair with the radio after lights off, a shared passion for music with a few close friends.

As well as local pirate music stations, I listened to shortwave broadcasters pumping out Cold War propaganda from far away. I was never lonely at night with these new voices drifting in from the ether. I penned letters to the BBC World Service and Radio Moscow which were read out across the world, passed the exams to become a ham radio operator, even built a radio transmitter.

The outside world began to impinge more. In the North, the civil rights movement of the 1960s had morphed into a murderous tit-for-tat war in the early 1970s. The corrupt reign of Taoiseach Charles Haughey was looming.

All that seemed far away at first. Adults didn't talk to children about the burning of the British embassy (which happened when I was eight) or the loyalist bombs in Dublin (when I was eleven). But, with time, it grew harder to avoid the turmoil. Children's programmes on BBC were forever being interrupted by appeals to keyholders to return to their premises; hours later, the evening news would show the bomb damage.

As a sixteen-year-old close to leaving school, I watched Taoiseach Charles Haughey's 'we are living way beyond our means' speech on television in January 1980. Looking around at the lumpy furniture, worn carpet and weary faces of my parents, I knew his reprimand could not apply to my hard-pressed family. Haughey, I decided, was the enemy.

With a friend, I started going to political meetings. We tried to produce a school magazine but the principal banned it. I attended protest marches, fascinated by the theatre involved – the banners, the chanting, the jostling for position among rival groups.

Amid this developing kaleidoscope of identities, my very early life hardly featured. I still professed little interest in this part of my past.

School hastened to a close. The games of chess in friends' houses and the never-ending kickabouts fell by the wayside as study took over. But study for what? My parents were desperate for me to go to college. They were convinced that university would provide me with the keys to society, the one they were locked out of, but they had little idea how that would come about. And neither had I.

School went from being an escape route to boring me. In the final months before the Leaving Certificate exams, I went on the mitch for the first time – a long solo cycle up the mountains. Sweating my way up the hills on my three-speed, I stopped once again at Killakee to look down on Dublin. My home was down there somewhere in the smoky haze, indistinguishable from all the other houses spreading out from the old core of the city. I could not wait to get away from it.

I kept going, on over the lonely Military Road crossing the Featherbeds. Stopping at Lough Bray – the same lake where Dad had turned around on his scooter years earlier – I went skinny-dipping, then sat on a rock to dry. What would the future bring, I wondered. I was nervous, but excited too. I had a thrilling feeling that part of my life was ending and another was about to begin. Though I felt the tug of home, I knew that things had to change.

A few of my classmates said they were hoping to study engineering after school; that was good enough for me. Nine months after I filled out my college entry form, I found myself in the back row of an enormous first-year class at Trinity College, wondering how I had got there. The first in my family to go to university. But was this me?

I retreated to the college canteen with the cheese sandwich and milk carton my mother had thrust in my hands that morning. I still didn't have a clue what career path I wanted to follow. All I did know was that there could be no going back. I had to make a go of this.

I was very naïve. During freshers' week, when new students are inducted into clubs and societies, some people asked me out to eat with them. I said yes, warily, because I had never eaten in a restaurant before. We walked to a nearby café, where a waiter handed us menus. Nothing on it made much sense to me but I chose the familiar chicken. When the food arrived, my dish was round and flat and lacked the leg I had expected to see. We were in a pizzeria but I did not know what pizza was. I ate quietly, copying others around the table. No-one suspected anything.

I threw myself into college life, joining societies, training with sports clubs, standing for class rep in the students' union. Though I still felt shy and awkward, I forced myself into situations where I had to meet new people or address groups. In my third year, I was elected to a full-time post in the union. My sabbatical year as education officer came with the perk of free rooms on the college campus, so I moved out of home.

When the coalition government removed the automatic entitlement of students to medical cards, we protested. There were the usual marches and petitions, but also occupations of public buildings.

A group of us occupied the offices of the Eastern Health Board on Thomas Street, rushing past bemused staff one morning to set up camp on the first floor. Banners were unfurled over the front of the building proclaiming the justice of our cause. Joe Duffy, firebrand leader of the Union of Students in Ireland (USI) and later popular broadcaster, brought in a megaphone to make speeches through the window to the passing traffic. It was all very exciting – and then it was dull.

We passed the time telling jokes and reading while waiting for something to happen. Friends came by with relief supplies – sleeping bags, food from the local chipper and Wispa bars. Like monks in a round tower, we hauled in these provisions by means of a bucket on a rope that we lowered from the front window.

The occupation dragged on for a few days and nights before some kind of face-saving exit strategy was worked out and we went home. I arrived back to rooms in college exhausted, to find my hedonistic flatmate in the throes of an extended party, having barely noticed my absence.

The campaign to have medical cards restored dragged on until a compromise was worked out. Naturally, we claimed victory but the entitlement to medical cards never came back.

I went home for Christmas. That New Year's Eve I stayed out all night at a party, returning home at lunchtime the following day with bloodshot eyes caused by ill-fitting contact lenses I had worn for too long.

My mother jumped to the inevitable conclusion. Just as she had done years before when I had my short-lived job as a lounge boy, she attacked me, physically and verbally.

Things had changed, though. For a start, I was much taller and stronger. Her attempted mauling had no impact on me; I caught hold of her flailing arms and put them to one side, and then moved away from her.

This time, I was not willing to put up with the assault. I had an easy out: the keys to my rooms in college jangled in my pocket. I told her she needed to apologise. When an apology failed to materialise, I walked out the door.

It felt strange to have left home so easily, but liberating too. The stand-off with Mam continued for more than a month before we sued for peace. I came back for lunch one weekend. Of the row, not a word was spoken. I resolved never to accept any further acts of violence. To her credit, they never happened again.

17

1984

Dad sits down across the table from me, brushing thin strands of hair over his crown with a shaky hand.

'Listen – your mother has been in contact.'

At first, I am confused. The words don't fit. Why is he talking about Mam when she is here in the kitchen with us? Then understanding begins to dawn on me. He hasn't paused before the word 'mother'. He doesn't do what Mam does, qualifying the M-word – talking about 'your mother who gave you up', 'your other mother', or much worse.

'She wants to see you.'

The conversation comes back to me with eerie clarity during my recuperation, despite the passage of years. I can see why – this moment marked the end of one phase of my life, from my adoption through childhood to the age of majority. The hard-won, tentative stability of those past two decades was about to be fractured. My understanding of who I was, and where I belonged, would be turned on its head.

I had just walked in the door after a long summer away. My hair long and unkempt, my arms peeling after months spent under a hot sun. Life was good. I had money in my pocket, earned sweeping the floors of the BMW factory in Munich. I holidayed for a few weeks, then took a language course in south-west France. My college lectures would be starting again shortly.

Going to the continent each summer while I was at university kept me away from home, and an increasingly vexed relationship with Mam. I put in long hours to earn the money that would buy my independence for the rest of the year. The work was dull – in other years I pickled sauerkraut in a huge vat and packed gherkins in jars – but the pay and overtime were good.

While I was abroad, I communicated with my parents by airmail letter. They didn't have a house phone. There wasn't even a public phone nearby. When calls had to be made, we asked the next-door neighbours for use of their phone. It was never a problem, but there was a limit to the conversation you were inclined to have in another person's hall while they were tucking in to their dinner in the adjoining kitchen.

Over that summer, Dad replied to my letters with his usual

mix of weather talk and local titbits. All was quiet. Nothing untoward was mentioned.

From the moment I arrive home, however, I sense the atmosphere has changed. Both my parents look haggard. They have aged visibly in the months I was away.

'Is there something wrong?'

There is barely time for a quick hug before Dad gestures for me to enter the kitchen.

'Everything is grand. Your dinner's ready in the oven. Sit down, son.'

They glance at each other stiffly as I take my usual place at the table. It doesn't take long for their worries to tumble out. Dad must have agreed beforehand to talk first.

'Your social worker came. A few months ago. She just knocked on the door.'

Social worker? What are they talking about?

'She gave you to us, when you were a baby. From the adoption agency. We hadn't seen her in years. We didn't know her from Adam when we opened the door.'

Mam takes over, resting her half-smoked cigarette on the edge of the draining board. 'Out of the blue, not so much as a by-your-leave. The cheek.'

Dad raises an arm to check his wife's commentary, in a rare act of authority. 'She couldn't ring us, I suppose, so she had to call by.'

'Did she never hear of a letter? We haven't moved.' Mam whips a tea towel from the back of the chair and uses it to serve up the hot plate with my dinner. Lamb chops in gravy, peas and chipped potatoes – not bad after a long trip home. I feel my stomach gurgling in anticipation of a square meal.

Cutting the meat, I try to make sense of what they are saying. It transpires that the social worker had turned up on my parents' doorstep over the summer. Mam and Dad were gardening out the back when the knock came.

I was familiar with the 'bad knock' from television. Someone is murdered, or killed in a traffic collision. Strangers in uniforms turn up on the front step wearing long faces, delivering bad news. But there were no gardaí or even strangers at their door on this Friday evening, just the woman who had handled my adoption years before. Her unannounced visit would upend all our lives.

I could imagine the shock on my parents' faces when the social worker arrived. Mam putting down the flowers she had cut in the garden, telling the woman to come in. Dad boiling the kettle for their unexpected guest.

The social worker, seemingly, arrived with a message from my birth mother. She wanted to see me.

When Dad imparts this information to me, I don't know how to respond. It is too much to take in. His words hang in the air for an age. A chunk of ash parts company with Mam's cigarette and drops to the floor. I start to cut up another chop while considering what to say. All I want is calm in the house. This turn of events will not lead to calm.

My parents sit down directly across from me, studying the

impact of their words. My mother testing me for loyalty, my father's heart aching.

'Of course, it's up to you to decide what you want to do. We won't stand in your way,' Dad says.

I see their eyes full of anticipated disappointment.

Her voice catching with emotion, my mother says, 'We will always love you.'

My mother doesn't tell me she loves me, not normally. From her words, I read: *My world will collapse if you do this to us*.

I look down at the plate, avoiding eye contact. 'This tastes good' is the best I can offer.

My parents' fear of losing me was groundless. Final papers for my adoption had been signed almost two decades previously. The laws defining their rights were clear and in their favour. Yet they continued to live in dread of the state swooping in to take away their cherished only child. The worry diminished with time, but was revived when the person who had handed me over to them, the incarnation of officialdom and 'the adoption machine', appeared on their doorstep like a revenant.

Up to this point, I had remained largely indifferent to the fact of my adoption. It was not something I thought about too often. The here-and-now always seemed to be too pressing to give it more consideration.

I knew others were interested in hearing about my unorthodox status. Other kids had cool hairstyles, sporting talent or good looks; I had a *dark secret*.

Friends, especially girls, were fascinated by my story. They wanted to know more, which required me to want to know more. Where was I born? Why had my genetic parents 'given me up'? Had I traced my birth mother?

These questions discomfited me. I did not have the answers. Neither was I inclined to dwell on them. There was space in my head for one mother only. Though my relations with Mam were well frayed by now, to even think about my birth mother felt like an act of deception.

One friend took a different line from the others, arguing that not knowing where you come from is a release. She claimed to be envious that adoption granted me a blank canvas on which I could draw my own design for life. I clung to this thought like a life raft, uncertain about what I really believed.

At this time, I was back living at home again, sleeping in my childhood bedroom and returning each evening from lectures to a home-cooked meat-and-two-veg, which might have been resting for hours under the grill.

Even as the parent of a young adult, Mam's parenting style yo-yoed constantly. One day, I was being treated like a child – 'Mind your purse down in that shopping centre. You never know what might happen.' The next, she was happy to grant me the generous freedoms I sought. While still a teenager, I headed off on long cycling trips around Ireland, then hitchhiked my way across Europe.

Overall, though, I decided in the days after learning of the social worker's visit, life was hard enough with one Irish mammy. I didn't need another one.

18

As I waited to see the social worker in the dark, wood-panelled confines of the adoption agency on South Anne Street, I wondered how often I had been brought here as a small child. Had I once crawled around on this well-worn carpet? Was my nappy changed on this table (unlikely!). Had I livened up these gloomy confines by bawling my head off? Perhaps, à la Flann O'Brien, some of my DNA had soaked into the armchair where I was now seated.

I was here with one aim: to restore normality at home. 'Thanks, but no thanks' would be my message. What I actually felt about the indirect approach from my birth mother didn't feature in my thinking.

Eventually, I was ushered into an inner office by a grey-haired woman in a demure skirt. This was my first meeting as an adult with the social worker who had arranged my adoption years before. A head's height above her, I moved awkwardly to meet the hand held out in greeting.

'My, aren't you a fine young lad?' she exclaimed. 'You've turned out well.' I forced myself not to smile; this woman was the enemy, I had convinced myself beforehand, because of the upset her visit to my parents had caused. I would say as little as possible, because to provide her with information would be a betrayal of my parents.

She offered me a cup of tea, which I declined. Then she asked me questions about myself and about my life up to this point. As she was speaking, I couldn't help thinking: this woman must have held me in her arms when I was a baby, before handing me over to Mam. Did she have a family of her own, I wondered, but dared not ask.

I tried to be guarded in my replies, but ended up talking more than I had intended. About my parents, and my relationship with them. I talked too about my studies, admitting I had no idea what the future held for me after I finished my degree.

The social worker was polite but business-like. Patting a firmly bound file on her desk, she said she was precluded for now from identifying my birth mother, but that could change if I agreed to have contact.

My mother had been in touch with the agency as I was growing up and once again after I turned eighteen, she explained. She lived outside Dublin. She'd had 'a few ups and downs' but was doing well now. She was very anxious to meet me.

I barely took in what she said to me, having rehearsed my lines beforehand. The agency should have made contact with me, not my parents, I said.

She waved away my complaint, saying my parents had over-reacted to her visit. She had visited them purely because they were the people she had dealt with before. Her call was simply a response to a 'human situation' caused by the contacts from my natural mother.

'Tell her I am doing fine,' I blurted out. 'Say I bear no ill-will towards her. But I am not ready to meet her. Not now.'

The woman just nodded. I thought I saw pity in her clear blue eyes. Was she judging me? Just how often did she have this kind of conversation?

My natural mother had travelled to England to have me, she explained, and had had little option but to return to Ireland to give me up for adoption because of the difficulty in placing children 'over there at the time'.

I bumbled on with thoughts of being conciliatory. 'Maybe at some point in the future ... when I'm older ... er, settled ... maybe then I'll be ready to meet her.'

The meeting couldn't end quickly enough for me. As soon as I could, I was descending the dark stairwell three steps at a time, careening towards the door and the bright, unencumbered world outside.

Thereafter, I returned to the life I knew, believing this would remain unchanged. How wrong I was.

I soon went back to college and my final year of engineering studies. Over Christmas, I began cramming for the exams.

One Friday evening in January, I went out for drinks with friends after the college library closed. I slept late the following morning. Coming to, I slowly made sense of the sounds around me: the familiar chatter of the birds under the eaves, a low moaning beyond the bedroom.

The moaning continued, but I still wasn't fully awake. What strange animal was making that noise below my window?

And then I knew, clarity dropping like a penny through a slot. Racing down the stairs, I found Dad collapsed outside the back door, his face ashen and his legs lying haphazardly on the ground. His glasses lay beside him, smashed on the hard concrete of the yard.

The moaning had lost its force now; it was more a quiet gurgling. I wiped a line of spit off his face with the back of my hand. Searching his dark eyes for some kind of a response, I pressed both my palms against his cheeks. Nothing.

There was no sign of my mother. She had gone down to the shops, a blameless trip she would rue for the rest of her life. I had no choice but to abandon Dad in order to raise the alarm. Barefoot and in my pyjamas, half-blind without my glasses, I raced to the next-door neighbour's house. No answer.

It was a pleasant winter's day, cotton-wool clouds minding their business in a blue sky, not that cold for January. Just another mundane morning on a quiet suburban street, until this happened. Alone in the open, I started to panic. Which neighbour to call on now? It had to be someone with a telephone. I headed down the end of the cul-de-sac, where one of the larger families lived. I reckoned that would increase the chance of someone answering the door; besides, the mother who lived there had trained as a nurse. Luckily, there was someone in. They called an ambulance.

The rest was a blur. Returning to Dad's side, I placed a cushion under his head. All I could find to cover him for warmth nearby was a tablecloth from the kitchen. The minutes ticked by. I chattered to him inanely, telling him over and over that things would be alright. I looked for a pulse, but could not find one. His stare was fixed on the sky above, the moaning had stopped and there was no sound at all coming from him. Already he seemed far away.

Now was the time to tell Dad that I loved him, but it wasn't the way we communicated, so I didn't.

After a long wait, the ambulance arrived. The paramedics took over, doing their compressions. Dad was placed on a stretcher and carried out of his home of almost thirty years. The team offered me a lift with him to the hospital. We left the road with sirens blazing, neighbours blessing themselves as we passed.

It didn't take long on a weekend morning to get to St James's Hospital, where he was rushed to the emergency department. But Dad was already dead.

The aftermath of his death was a jumble. The days of crying. The unwanted spotlight as a chief mourner at his funeral Mass. One person after another telling me they were 'sorry for your troubles'. The priest and his pat sermon. A burial on a bleak mountainside graveyard above the city, dogs barking in nearby kennels. Below smog blanketing the housing estates of south Dublin where I had grown up. For months, a knot inside. Feeling like a small boy, adrift in life without a father.

19

Three months after breaking my back, I returned full-time to working as a news editor at *The Irish Times*. This role was desk-based. I didn't have to undertake assignments in the field, which might have tested my stamina. However, the job of overseeing the flow of news stories each day is highly pressurised, and it continues around the clock. It also involves a lot of sitting.

I got quickly into the swing of things. The work was as stimulating as ever. After the isolation of sick leave, it was great to be part of a team once more. But there were also rough days, when my body didn't feel up to sitting at a desk all day, when thumping waves of pain deep within blotted out my ability to focus on the screen in front of me. Sometimes, I took lying-down breaks on the floor of the office; other times, I cadged painkillers from colleagues to get me through the day's work.

My employer had said to take as long as I needed, to work part-time at first, acclimatise. Now I wondered if I'd been too keen for a swift return to normality.

Back at home, I found myself thinking a lot about my father, for the first time in many years. I also wondered why I had passed up the initial chance to meet my birth mother, the woman who had brought me into the world. Why had I not acceded to her simple wish to meet, when I knew she must have gone through tremendous heartbreak on losing contact with her child two decades before?

I was young back then, I supposed, and wrapped up in myself. Emotionally a bit numb perhaps. Though I'd professed to have views on all sorts of things, in fact I had never really thought through the issues around my own adoption.

I was spooked at how rattled Mam and Dad were by the visit of my social worker, and wary of my mother's mood swings. Anything that threatened to disrupt the delicate equilibrium at home was to be avoided.

For my parents, disaster was always around the corner, malign forces conspiring to wrong them. Keeping their heads down was a way of life.

The dull flop of a bill arriving through the letterbox could ruin a morning. How much? Do we have enough? What will happen if we don't? I would try to explain that the money wasn't due for another fortnight. That there would always be a reminder if the bill went unpaid. No dice: purses were emptied and hiding places raided for spare cash to raise the amount due. I would be dispatched to the post office with the precise sum, down to the last penny, that was required to settle the debt.

After his business collapse years earlier, Dad was incapable of swallowing financial shocks. Even minor setbacks hit him hard. I remember telling him once that my bike had been stolen. As a teenager, I was always having bikes stolen. On hearing the news over the dinner table, he let out a piercing cry. Recoiling on the chair, he clutched his heart alarmingly, as though he had been shot or was suffering cardiac arrest. The loss of the bike represented a month's earnings, at a time when he didn't have a regular income. In his catastrophising cry, I heard a lifetime's insecurities and humiliations.

Mam deluded herself with dreams of imagined riches around the corner. There was the uncle who plied the cattle boats between Ireland and Argentina and was said by her to own half the cattle in South America. Another branch of the family had gone from Donegal to South Africa, apparently, and owned a diamond mine. 'There's plenty of them left for all of us if we go down there,' she told anyone who would listen.

Mam could have a sharp tongue, but she was a sucker for a sad story. She found it hard to turn away door-to-door sellers offering to sell rugs or sharpen knives without buying something from them. She never hesitated to give money to the women in shawls who arrived regularly at her door, offering to pray for her to Mary, mother of God and all the saints.

My parents were easy prey for the grifters who thrived in a marginal economy. One year, they saved up to buy a second-hand car from a local garage. Having agreed a price, they handed over the cash to the owner of the garage. He told them the car needed a few final adjustments; they should come and pick it up the following morning. When they arrived at the garage the following day, they found he had fled to England with the car.

The aftermath of my dad's death was dominated by the need to make practical arrangements. Mam had to sell his car and pawn her rings to help pay for the funeral. There wasn't time to grieve properly, or to think about our relationship.

Later, however, I found myself evaluating his legacy. Despite his passivity, Dad influenced me greatly. Though, of course, I never told him, I hugely admired his gentleness, modesty and basic decency and wanted to model those in my personality. He showed me how work helps to put a person's life on an even keel, and not just financially. Dad never made much money, and perhaps he should have pushed harder for his due, but work anchored him.

He was a tradesman who got his hands dirty for a living. Both he and Mam left school early. Did that make me working class? I wasn't certain.

My mother came from generations of butchers, my father from a long line of house-painters. I was the first in my family to study at third level. They were desperately short of money throughout my upbringing. Teabags were reused, two-ply tissues were separated to make them last longer. We had motorised transport, but only just – a Lambretta scooter, followed by an

NSU Prinz followed by the ancient Morris Minor Traveller. My father was chronically unemployed, or under-employed, in his years of decline, as I was growing up. After suffering painful injuries in a car crash, he went on disability benefit.

Our family never went out. The only holiday I had was when Mam took me with her on the ferry to visit an aunt in Oldham. I grew up insecure about money, because I was raised in a home where there was never enough. I remember many anxious conversations between my parents at the kitchen table, where they dissected their lack of means in pencilled lists of tiny incomings and outgoings; the sums never balanced properly.

And yet, I never lacked much. Meanwhile, other factors were tugging me up the social ladder. My parents owned their house, for example. That gave them a foothold in the middle classes, something I could build on. In buying a house in the suburbs, they had distanced themselves from their working-class roots, aside from occasional visits to relatives. They were, I think, the only inner-city Dubliners on their road.

Despite the small size of our family, our fridge was always heaving: bagged assortments of meat, from sausages and black pudding to the roast for the coming Sunday; foil-wrapped boxes of Galtee and Calvita cheese; tomatoes and heads of butter lettuce for salad; bowls of soggy trifle; my mother's weekly bottle of stout.

'You never know who is going to call in,' Mam would explain. No-one ever did, aside from the usual neighbourhood women calling over for a cup of tea and a gossip. The men of the area stayed at home or socialised in the pub, but my dad didn't do pubs. My parents never entertained and they were never invited to other people's houses for dinner.

Years later, visiting the house of a college friend from a comfortable background, I opened the fridge and found it virtually empty. Her parents were professionals, yet never felt the need to fill their fridge with food 'just in case'. What on earth, I worried, did they eat?

20

In the mid-1980s, I discovered I had a heart murmur. The news came as a surprise to me. The only reason I was seeing a doctor was because I had come through a job interview and the company wanted me to be examined before offering me a position. I didn't even want the job – though I was quite happy to take the paid flights to London for the interview and subsequent medical.

And now I was being told that, despite feeling in the best of health, I had a potentially serious medical issue. In my early twenties, I was suddenly confronted with the conundrum experienced by many adoptees, of not knowing my medical history.

Medical reasons are often cited by adopted people as a reason for seeking more information about their origins. Some simply want to gain a greater insight into their health background through contact with birth parents. Other have worries about specific inherited genetic conditions.

Up to this point, I hadn't been that bothered. I was young

and fit. I suspect I was also loath to learn anything negative about my health. I did ask Mam about the doctor's findings but she knew nothing about it.

The murmur played a crucial role in my early life, and features prominently in my adoption file, but I wasn't to know this for many years. 'This child has a slight heart murmur and cannot be recommended for adoption at present,' a London hospital doctor determined shortly after I was born.

My medical disability was a bar to adoption but clearly not to my removal from England. Perhaps I could be placed in a nursery or foster home in Dublin while my health was being reviewed, the doctor suggested, though he must have known I would receive better attention in London than in Dublin.

My adoptive parents were left in the dark about the medical issues of the child they were receiving. After learning of the murmur, I put it to the back of my mind, and the question of medical tests on the long finger. But I did wonder what else was to be discovered about my past.

After Dad's death, I wanted nothing to do with the adoption agency. Yet the seed had been planted; from this point on, the fact of my adoption loomed larger in my life. Though I had spurned my birth mother's request for contact, I now knew more about her than I ever had. It was harder to ignore her needs. She had been trying to contact me for years. I found out much later that, when I was growing up with my adoptive parents, she wrote regularly to the adoption agency. How was I? How was my health? Could she see me?

The social workers always wrote back with soothing words of reassurance, whether they were justified or not. I was 'in marvellous form', 'a great little fellow in every way' and a 'great favourite with other children'. They were gilding the lily – or worse – but I wouldn't find this out until much later.

As required by law, the agency firmly ruled out any meeting between me and my birth mother once my adoption had been legally formalised. Still the letters came from her each year. Was I making my Holy Communion? Could she send a birthday card? Could she look me up when I turned eighteen?

She could, and didn't waste any time contacting the adoption agency once I became an adult. That led to the fateful visit to my adoptive parents I described earlier, which had a profound and troubling impact on them.

Though I had parked the issue of getting in touch with my birth mother, Mam, ironically, kept it on the agenda. Her attacks grew ever wilder as I reached the age where this contact could be made. She was a hussy, a tramp, a go-about-town, she assured me, a woman who had wasted her prime gadding about. Someone who couldn't be bothered to look after the son she bore when I needed her most. And who was seeking to dig her claws into me now that the hard work of rearing a child was done.

Whenever I was in trouble with Mam for some misdemeanour, real or imagined, it was ascribed to my genes. 'You'll never come to much – just like your feckin' mother,' I remember her snarling at me once.

I learned not to tread this territory. It was better not to ask questions about where I had come from or to express any interest in tracing my birth mother. To do so was to risk my mother blowing another gasket, while my father fruitlessly tried to calm matters.

Mam wasn't like this all the time, or even much of the time. Yet, as with any volcanic eruption, there was a lead-in and an aftermath to her outbursts, during which a grimness hung in the air. This prelude, and the anxious churn it caused in my tummy, was often worse than the actual moment of explosion.

Invariably – inevitably – once relieved of her frustrations, Mam would dissolve into tears, hug me tight and apologise profusely. 'It's only because I love you so much' became her mantra. She did love me, I knew it, and I loved her back, but these words lost their sheen as her explode-and-repent behaviour was repeated over and over.

Following Dad's premature death, years passed before I visited the adoption agency again. At the time I first declined to meet my birth mother, I was a student living at home. Strict rules were in place preventing information being passed about either birth mother or adoptee without the consent of both sides. Apart from the fact that she lived outside Dublin, I knew nothing about her, not even her name. Not that I asked. I had kept the door ajar, though, telling the agency I might be ready for contact at some time in the future.

When Dad died, there wasn't much time to wallow in my loss. My final exams at university were imminent. He left no savings, and we had no car now that Mam had sold it. Still, there were just two of us. Mam and I didn't need much. I was able to live off the small stipend from my government college grant and the money I had saved from working abroad during the summer. Mam got by on the widow's pension.

I passed the exams and got my degree. After the graduation ceremony, I took her out for a meal in a city-centre hotel, just the two of us. Biting into the food, she broke a tooth. We both laughed, still happy to be marking the day.

I was free to go now, and had long planned to. But now that the moment had arrived, something held me back. I felt guilty about the prospect of leaving her on her own, certainly, but it was more than that. We had lived together so long, so completely in thrall to each other's emotions, it felt extremely difficult to leave. So I lingered on at home for months, no longer a child but not yet a rounded adult.

21

I could feel the letter burning a hole in my pocket as I walked out of the adoption agency and down the street in search of a café. Two neatly folded sheets of Basildon Bond paper – a first message from the hitherto parallel universe occupied by my birth mother.

June 1989, and it was about time. I should have been feeling excited, and a bit nervous – instead, I was angry. The letter, the first she sent to me, had languished in the adoption agency for more than a year. The agency was well used to receiving letters from my birth mother, but this was the first time she had addressed one to me. I was an adult, and she was entitled to communicate with me through the agency, provided I was agreeable.

However, staff elected, after internal deliberation, not to pass it on. It was better to 'leave matters as they are' until I requested contact, my birth mother was told. The ball was left in my court, though I didn't know it. The letter remained in my file in South Anne Street until I happened to make a chance visit the following year.

By now, I had moved abroad. Ireland was in the doldrums yet again when I finished college in 1985. My generation, once dubbed the 'Young Europeans' for our marketable skills in science and engineering, were leaving in droves. My entire electronic engineering class emigrated – to Germany, The Netherlands, the US and the UK. I took a job in Switzerland the following year, once Mam had recovered somewhat from the death of her husband of nearly forty years.

For the first time in my life, I had a proper job. I remitted some of my wages to support Mam and pay off the small outstanding amount on my parents' mortgage. My new role as a benefactor helped salve any guilt pangs I felt over my absence.

In her widowhood, she got to live a little. A cousin in England brought her over for yearly visits, and she applied for her first passport so she could come to see me in Switzerland. She looks chuffed in the snaps I took of her on Alpine passes and before flower-bedecked chalets. In restaurants, she chatted away to strangers, most of whom spoke no English, while I worked out the German for lamb chops and mashed potatoes.

I was now, indubitably, a grown-up. I was living independently and earning my own keep. It was time to stop acting like a dependant, taking my cue from Mam in relation to my birth mother. Separately, the commitment I had previously made to contact my birth mother at some date in the future weighed upon me. I resolved to call in to the adoption agency the next time I was home and discuss the possibility of contact with my birth mother.

The meeting was for the most part cordial; I was, apparently, transformed, 'all sweetness and light and very open and friendly', the social worker recorded in her notes.

If this was true, I imagine it was down to my changed circumstances. No longer penniless and financially dependent at home, or frustrated with conservative Ireland, I was now living in cosmopolitan Geneva.

I recited my current situation: how my father had died a few years earlier and I was now living abroad. I said I still wasn't sure about contacting my birth mother. The social worker explained how my natural mother 'always felt upset and guilty' because she had parted with me for adoption. She then handed me the letter.

It felt confusing to have something so tangible from my birth mother in my hand. Up to this point, she had been an abstraction; now, through this short letter, she felt real. And that was before I read its contents.

I found a quiet café where I could give time to reading the letter. Opening the envelope, I spread the sheets of writing paper flat on the table. My eyes went first to the signature at the bottom. There, in plain blue cursive, was the name of the woman who bore me.

Olive.

I'd never known an Olive.

The letter was short, the tone almost apologetic.

Dear Paul,
I am writing to you hoping you are well and that perhaps you will write back. I have been in touch with the Adoption Agency and they told me some details of you.

Perhaps we could meet sometime and we could talk. They told me from the adoption agency that they gave you some knowledge of me and that you called in to them.

I am now 51 years old and not really in very good health but I feel that it might benefit us both if we became reconciled with one another. I hope that your adoptive parents are well.

That is all I have to say for now.
With best wishes and hoping to hear from you soon.
(Mrs) Olive Scully

So few words on which to form a judgement. But the reference to ill-health fazed me. Perhaps my birth mother was looking for emotional and physical support I would be unable to give. Then I reread the suggestion for us to be 'reconciled with one another'.

How could I be reconciled with someone I had never known and had never chosen to leave? That stuck in the craw but it also gave a convenient reason to back away. The truth was,

I wasn't ready to meet her. Mam was still prominent in my thinking, and life was turbulent enough already.

Through the adoption agency, I palmed my birth mother off once again. Perhaps, I said, we could write to each other, and then think about meeting. In the future, sometime.

The adoption agency failed to contact Olive as I had suggested, and I did nothing to follow up. I put the letter aside and forgot about it. My birth mother remained a name, nothing more. My life was more intense than ever – there were new jobs, friends and relationships. The rollercoaster of the present was infinitely more attractive than a murky meander through the past.

22

1990

Switzerland was great, but it wasn't home. After five years living there, I returned to Ireland. As with many emigrants, I found the experience of living overseas had forced me to think more about who I was. From far away, I made peace with my home country. Having seen the flaws of other countries, I became more accepting of Ireland's.

In truth, I had missed aspects of living in Ireland. Was it the ever-changing weather, the calming proximity of the sea, the relative lack of materialism? At home, you didn't have to have a registration plate for your bicycle, as I did in Switzerland, and you weren't required to vacate the balcony of your flat for a 10 p.m. curfew.

It was time to test the waters in Dublin. I rented a flat near the Grand Canal (sharing with a friend who was to die tragically in a car crash a few years later). I would never again live permanently at home with my mother, but at least I could be around for her as she grew old.

That autumn, I enrolled in a postgraduate course in journalism. The move represented a belated expression of rebellion. My parents had always held what they called 'the gutter press' in low regard. They had more time for the quality press but tabloids were, my mother reminded me, 'full of smut'.

Still, they bought an evening paper most days as I was growing up, along with a couple of the Sundays from a stall outside Mass. I read them avidly. Initially, the sports coverage at the back grabbed my attention, but I quickly developed an interest in domestic and international news. My parents thought it improper to talk about politics – they were pretty apolitical themselves.

The guts of a decade had passed between the end of school and me starting to train as a journalist. Mam still disapproved of my choice of career but by then I was financially independent and living away from home. Her influence on me had waned.

Back in Dublin, it was harder to push from my mind all those awkward questions about my origins. And just as I returned, society was ramping up its fascination with adoption.

Though more than 100,000 Irish children were born outside marriage between the 1920s and the mid-1970s, the issue was seldom mentioned when I was growing up. 'It was a taboo subject, never discussed in polite company and, if mentioned at all, then only in hushed tones of holy indignation. An appalling stigma attached to "illegitimacy". Having a child outside marriage was regarded as an unspeakably scandalous act,' wrote journalist Mike Milotte in *Banished Babies*, his exposé of the illegal baby export trade, published in 1997.

Vestiges of that stigma hung around for decades. Up to 1970, for example, an 'illegitimate' person could not join An Garda Síochána. Illegitimacy was a disqualification for the priesthood until 1983. As late as 1984, a woman garda was found to be in breach of discipline after becoming pregnant out of wedlock. Only in 1987, when I was in my twenties, was the status of illegitimacy abolished.

The size of the stigma depended on where you were in society. 'The "higher up" the social scale you were considered to be, the greater the shame in having a baby outside marriage was,' social worker Anne Ronayne was quoted as saying in an Adoption Authority of Ireland report in 2024. 'If a girl's father was a professional, like a doctor or a solicitor, she absolutely would not want any of her family to know about it. Similarly, if, for example, a Garda got a girl pregnant, he'd be in terrible trouble with the Gardaí.'

If society didn't want to know about extra-marital births, it remained perennially curious about adoption. I knew this because of how it affected the mood in our house. The country's leading broadcaster, Gay Byrne, covered the subject regularly on his daily radio programme as I was growing up. Byrne would often read out anguished letters from women who had given up a child for adoption, or equally forlorn letters from adult adoptees searching for their birth parents.

My mother listened to these heart-rending stories standing at her kitchen sink, looking out at the garden. Her back was turned against me, so I couldn't see her face. I felt something change in her upon hearing these sad tales. A heavy silence would fall over the house in their aftermath. Her mood for the rest of the day would become unpredictable. I learned it was best to steer clear of her until it improved.

The other end of this three-legged adoption stool – the adoptive parent – featured only rarely in the emotion-tugging narratives served up on radio chat shows. But even if Gay Byrne had shouted from the heights about the challenges faced by people like my mother, I don't think she would have welcomed it. Like most people, I suppose, she wanted to fit in, not to be told how she was different, how she hadn't given birth to any children.

My views on these accounts of separation and heartbreak were strongly coloured by their impact on Mam. Far from being sympathetic towards birth mothers, I grew defensively supportive of my mother and the position of adoptive mothers collectively. In the great debate between the rights of birth mothers and adoptive mothers that played out in my head, I was decisively in favour of adoptive mothers. I didn't have the emotional bandwidth to realise you could be sympathetic to the plight of both.

Shortly after I returned to live in Ireland, controversy erupted over plans by a developer to redevelop the site of a Magdalene laundry in the north Dublin suburb of Drumcondra, where the bodies of over 150 former inmates were exhumed. Critics said the plans were disrespectful and there were calls for the women's experience to be memorialised.

Magdalene asylums or laundries in Dublin date back to 1767. The first was established by a Protestant philanthropist but the Catholic Church began opening their own asylums from the 1840s on, in response to proselytising by Protestant institutions.

I didn't know much about this part of Irish history, but learned more as new revelations came to light. The Magdalene institutions, effectively workhouses where 'fallen women' were forced to work without pay, continued to operate in Ireland for decades after they had closed in other countries. Between 1922 and 1996, about 10,000 women and girls passed through ten Irish Magdalene laundries run by Catholic religious orders in Dublin and other cities and towns. Conditions were harsh, food was basic and life was subject to strict rules.

The Magdalene laundries and mother and baby homes became 'synonymous with the establishment of a narrow moral code, a preoccupation with sex and the virtual equation of immorality with sexual immorality', according to historian J.J. Lee, writing in 1989. The last Magdalene laundry closed as recently as 1996.

As Ireland changed in the 1990s, the Magdalene controversy sparked a wider examination of the control apparatus developed by the Catholic Church to deal with awkward social problems and to police morality through much of the twentieth century. This system, which has been described as 'coercive confinement', included the Magdalene laundries, industrial schools and mother and baby homes – the common thread being unmarried mothers or their children.

Magdalene institutions, I learned, focused on women who were deemed to be 'fallen' or 'immoral'. This included women considered to be prostitutes or mentally ill, but also those who were known to have engaged in pre-marital sex or were deemed troublesome by their families. Mother and baby homes were primarily concerned with keeping out of the public eye unmarried women who were pregnant. Key to this was the removal of their babies, primarily through the adoption process.

I had read Paddy Doyle's harrowing account of growing up in an industrial school in *The God Squad* and Mannix Flynn's *Nothing to Say*, an account of the time he spent in industrial schools, including Letterfrack, where he had been abused. I came to know Paddy when we were neighbours in Dublin, though I never mentioned my own background in talking to him.

At the time, I never saw this slice of history as part of a continuum that connected with me. I had grown up in the relative comfort of an adoptive family home, rather than a harsh institution. Repeatedly told to feel grateful for where I had landed, I didn't know anything about my life prior to adoption.

From this time, there were regular journalistic exposés of the trauma suffered by the survivors of Magdalene laundries, industrial schools and mother and baby homes. Ultimately, separate state investigations were established into each of these sets of institutions. Successive governments issued apologies, however belatedly. Collectively, society expressed contrition.

There was less focus on legal adoptions. Adoptees, and adoptive parents, were expected to be happy for their placements. 'Aren't you lucky your mam and dad took you in?' one well-meaning neighbour once told me.

Equally, birth parents who had given children up for adoption were considered fortunate to have dodged the bullet of institutional care and were often advised to move on with their lives.

But as more information trickled out, it was clear that not all adoptions were straightforward. Some involved the forced removal of children from their mothers. Others involved illegal registrations of children. Thousands of babies had been exported to the US. In 1996, the state admitted that false names had been supplied for the birth certificates of some children adopted in the 1950s and 1960s. For this reason, amongst others, many mothers died without discovering what had become of their forsaken children.

Even legal adoptions, such as my own, involved huge secrecy. The role of adoption agencies as gate-keepers for this system was coming under increasing scrutiny. Many of these arrangements came to be regarded as forced adoptions. It was becoming clear that adoption, Irish-style, was a lot more complex than had been portrayed.

Six years passed before, in 1995, I returned to the adoption agency. Having given renewed thought to my birth mother's approach, I told them I was ready to 'tread carefully and cautiously' on establishing contact.

'Paul doesn't seem to have any hang-ups at all now, contrary to what he had about eleven years ago' was the social worker's verdict this time. 'He seems very up-front and straightforward about his adoption. He would like to know something about his origins, but he is concerned about his birth mother's expectations and what reopening this situation may mean for him.'

My mother could be dead by now, she warned, while offering to make 'some enquiries'. Finally, after delays on both sides, the first steps were being taken to put me in touch with Olive.

23

I never told Mam what I was planning. I couldn't face her jealous grief if she knew I had been in touch with the agency that had arranged my adoption. Worse, that I had initiated this contact.

By the mid-1990s, her health had begun a slow decline due to respiratory problems linked to her years of smoking. Her cognitive abilities remained as sharp as ever, but as the years passed, she needed to be hospitalised regularly for progressively longer periods. Eventually, she needed supplemental oxygen at home in order to breathe comfortably. She still managed to trundle up to daily Mass, pushing the canister in its cart.

It might have been easier for her if I had moved back home, but I had decided this would not be good for either of us. With a little distance, we got on fine. And with the help of good neighbours, we coped with her mounting health issues.

After completing the master's course, I started to make a living as a freelance journalist, writing for a variety of newspapers and magazines. I wasn't living at home, but I visited Marian

Grove regularly. Occasionally, Mam would test my loyalty by quizzing me about contacts with the adoption agency and 'her'. My approach was to say I had heard nothing – which was true, mostly – and then switch the subject.

Life became increasingly difficult as her health declined. Living alone, she had plenty of time for late-life rumination. On bad days, she threw out once-treasured mementos, sometimes so violently I had to clean up the fragments afterwards. Photos were torn up, or ripped from their frames, and ornaments broken. She took a scissors or knife to one photograph of a family get-together, carefully cutting one of her in-laws out of the picture, leaving the rest of us smiling on either side of a blank space. As usual, the focus of her ire was a woman. The relative who suffered this airbrushing had always seemed a gentle enough person to me. I could not understand why Mam had become so angry with her.

When I eventually made the decision to seek a meeting with my birth mother, I requested 'complete confidentiality' on the form I sent to the adoption agency, underlining the words, as if that would make a difference.

The legal position on the provision of birth information to adoptees was confirmed by a test case that came before the Supreme Court in the late 1990s. While every child had a constitutional right to know the identity of their natural parents, unmarried mothers who had given up their children also had a right to privacy. If they chose to exercise this right, there was no possibility of contact, except in individual cases through the courts. But without knowing their birth mother's name, adopted people could not obtain their birth certificate, even though this existed as a public document and was theoretically accessible to anyone.

On foot of the court's decision, the attorney general advised that the Oireachtas could not legislate to allow unrestricted access to birth cases, because this would not pay sufficient regard to privacy rights. The constitution would have to be amended if this access were to be allowed.

Years before, when my birth mother first got in touch, I was living at home. I might have been old enough to vote, but I enjoyed no privacy. Now I owned my first house, a tiny two-up, two-down in the Liberties area of inner-city Dublin. I didn't need to intercept the mail before anyone saw it, as I used to do in the family home. All the same, I remember taking care to ensure there were no stray letters left lying around whenever my mother was due to visit.

Appointed to the staff of *The Irish Times* in 1993, I was to stay over thirty years with the newspaper, moving around between different reporting roles. In all that time, I hardly ever wrote about adoption. Indeed, I seldom wrote about myself, except in a sporting context – for example, when I ran the Dublin marathon. I think this was no accident. I did not want to run the risk of my birth mother putting two and two together from any personal information and unilaterally making contact with me.

Mam finally warmed to my career in journalism. Neighbours she considered her betters had begun referring in conversation to articles I had written. In order to find out what they were talking about, she was forced to purchase copies of *The Irish Times*, a newspaper that had never before appeared in our house. She took to perusing copies in the newsagent's. If I had a front-page story, she would buy a copy and take it with her on visits to her neighbours, where she would point out the article to friends. Unless, of course, it concerned a disapproved-of subject, such as divorce or abortion.

I was touched by her interest, even if it was clear that the actual newspaper was seldom opened. Once, she bought an edition that had a crease through one of my articles due to some minor fault in the printing process. All that would satisfy her was to whip out the iron and remove the blemish on her son's writing. For all that, I don't think she read the article.

I had to wait after my initial contact with the agency. It took months to get an appointment, but I was also dragging my heels. I was still feeling strangely disconnected. All sorts of wild thoughts ran through my mind. What if my birth mother was an oddball? What if she wanted something from me? How would I cope with the fallout from a meeting? I proposed a roundabout form of communication through the agency. Olive was told to write to me through it. When they received her letter, staff summoned me to pick it up in their office. Back at home, I then wrote my reply, which was delivered to her through the agency.

It was a laborious arrangement. After the long years of waiting, the delay must have been unbearable for her.

In her letters, Olive told me about her family and work, and made passing reference to earlier events. I was born in London, she confirmed, and my father had been a garda – not a profession that ever featured in Mam's tales about my parentage. He had later moved to England, she intimated, and was living there when she last heard from him.

Far from looking forward to meeting my birth mother, my concern over 'two-timing' the two mothers in my life verged on paranoia. I had nightmares about being caught out, and of Mam accusing me of betrayal. Mary's central place in my life was secure, I knew that. She had raised me, influenced me hugely, loved me with almost every fibre of her being. But I also knew she wouldn't see it that way were I to tell her of my contact with Olive or, worse, were she to uncover this treachery through a slip-up on my part.

The hiatus before my planned meeting with Olive allowed me time to daydream. The adopted person who knows nothing about a birth mother is free to imagine a life for her. Walking down a crowded street, passing a thousand strangers, you realise that any woman of roughly the right age and race could be the mother who bore you. She could be living around the corner, unbeknownst to you, or on the other side of the world. She could be beautiful, rich, accomplished, lucky – or none of these.

And with the woman you conjure up in your imagination goes an imagined back story. How she was a famous scientist who dedicated her life to battling a rare disease, only to succumb to it herself. How your entire family was wiped out in a tragic car crash, except for you.

What if my birth mother were famous, and I got dragged along in the slipstream of celebrity? I dreamed how my life would be changed by this kind of discovery – for the better, naturally.

My wild conjectures never extended to my birth father. He remained off-camera, a vaguely sinister presence. Years would pass before the need grew to learn more about him.

My mother had lobbed into the mix her own shards of imagined biography for my birth mother: how she had been 'forced' to give me up, having come from a 'good family', or how I was the product of a doomed love affair. The adoption agency had passed on these snippets to her, she suggested, notwithstanding the legal ban on providing such information. But the stories she told changed over the years, so I had my doubts.

24

May 1996

I walk up to the prearranged meeting point, nervous as a horse at the starting gate. The time has finally arrived to meet my mother, and I suddenly feel very out of place. A confirmed city-dweller, I find myself in a busy provincial town; a tourist in my own country.

The day had dawned bright and breezy, the threat of rain never far away. Driving my ageing Ford Fiesta out of Dublin, I tried to sort out the jumble of thoughts in my head. It was strange to be making this journey, after all the years of refusal and procrastination on my part and the delays dealing with the agency. But it also felt timely, given that the two of us had started corresponding over previous months.

Familiar city streets quickly gave way to green fields and glossy hedgerows. I was leaving my comfort zone, physically as well as mentally.

Though I knew the road west from countless weekend jaunts

to the Atlantic coast, this trip was different. I was travelling only as far as Athlone, where my mother was staying. I hadn't seen the town since I was a teenager and the bus bringing our class back from the pope's youth Mass in Galway made a toilet stop by the Shannon.

My mission remains clandestine. No-one knows I am in touch with this stranger. More lies and secrets to layer upon the ones first kept over thirty years before. I'm sure my mother remembers the last time she saw me, but I am effectively meeting her for the first time.

I had agonised all morning. Was this a celebration, or a solemn occasion? What should I be feeling on such a day? How would I be received? What does a grown adult wear, meeting his mother for the first time?

I opted to dress for comfort on this summer's day: short-sleeved shirt, cargo pants, a daypack on my back. On the drive, I worried that my casual choice of clothes betrayed a lack of respect, or showed I wasn't taking the encounter seriously. The next moment, my thoughts flip-flopped; another, sterner voice inside whispering that this meeting had little to do with me and my life, that it was just a quick link-up with someone from my distant past. It was merely a box to be ticked on a bucket list of life tasks. My birth mother had asked to see me; well, here I was.

Pausing before the imposing doors of the hotel where we had arranged to meet, residents and other guests scurrying past me, I consider turning on my heels. If I leave now, my anonymity will remain intact. I can go on with life as it was. I can continue to look Mary, the mother who raised me, straight in the eye. I can remain that blank slate my friend had talked about, free to forge my own destiny without the obvious influence of blood ties.

To push open those doors is to leave one enclosed world – the familiar surroundings of my upbringing and notions of family – and establish a bridge to another, as yet unknown, environment, with who knows what consequences. There can be no going back.

Yet the very fact I am here says something. Now that inner voice is urging me on through the doors of the hotel. The quickfire quiz round rattles on in my head. I know I'm not completely satisfied with the life I've been leading. I am a little curious about the stranger waiting for me inside. And I do owe it to my birth mother to show my face. After all, she might help me fill in some of the blanks. Tell me who my father is.

As I stand marooned on the pavement, my head filled with these contradictory thoughts, I realise just how much these questions have weighed on the margins of my mind. With a pang of guilt I remember Olive's earlier wish to meet. She was getting older and had some health problems. It is possible she felt guilty over her decision to place me for adoption. A meeting will help her too. I take a deep breath and push open the doors.

25

The lobby is half-empty. No-one I can see by the reception desk looks like they are waiting to meet a long-lost child. Panicking slightly, I veer into the adjoining restaurant, which is packed with locals tucking into their carvery lunches.

My eyes scan the room. Most of the tables are occupied by diners huddled in gossiping clumps over well-filled plates. Not them.

I breathe out. Slight relief. Maybe she's decided not to come. Maybe I can leave now and go back to Dublin. Surely I belong to nobody.

And then I see her, down the end of the room, far from the crowd. A lone woman sitting at a small table.

Olive.

Silver-haired, round-faced, solid, wearing a thin raincoat despite the heat, her hands clasped stiffly before her on the table, her head bowed over a pot of tea.

My mother. The woman who bore me. Yet not my mother.

Lunchtime is ending and the place is emptying out. I stride up to her wearing my best smile, then falter.

'Olive,' I whisper, almost apologetically. 'It's me.'

She rises slowly, greeting my hyper-original introduction with a solemn look. The first thing I notice are the lines on her face. Then her eyes: alert, blue, tired. She clasps a cardigan she is carrying with one hand and shakes my hand with the other. We give each other an approximation of a hug, an awkward angling of arms held too far out. No kisses, no high emotion, definitely no tears. I drop my pack onto an adjoining chair and we sit down.

Olive moves her hands to her lap, kneading one palm against the other, as though nervous. She fixes her gaze on the table, making eye contact difficult.

'You look like a German.'

'I've been away a bit alright,' I reply, my initial surprise at her remark morphing into a laugh. I understand how the gangly, bespectacled man sitting opposite her might as well be a foreign tourist as far as she is concerned. Viewed from my side of the table, too, the gulf between us is as wide as the nearby Shannon. 'Some of the travelling must have rubbed off on me. It's – it's good to see you.'

'And you. You must be awful tall.'

'I am, it's true. But you're tall enough yourself – I think.'

And so the two of us, strangers, circle each other cautiously. Both of us find it hard to get away from the small talk: the weather, our journeys here, what we had done so far this year. Or maybe we feel more comfortable in that space.

I offer up a potted version of my life so far, quickly triggering descriptive landmines.

'I grew up near Dublin. Mam – I mean, Mary – didn't work but Dad was a painter. Not an artist-painter, a house-painter.'

And later: 'My mother and father were both from Dublin.'

Olive doesn't baulk or react to these awkward references. Far from it: she seems ready to accept a subordinate rank in the motherhood league, at least insofar as it applies to me. Anyway, the mentions are deliberate; to describe Mary and Pat as my adoptive parents – anything other than simply *my parents* – would be disloyal, I had decided.

I explain that I had a good upbringing and that she does not need to feel guilty for giving me up when I was a baby. She looks at me strangely as I babble about how Ireland was an unforgiving place in the 1960s, particularly for unmarried mothers.

Every so often, she lobs in a direct, unexpected question. 'Do you go to Mass every week?' she interjects as I am talking about my education. She says nothing when I tell her that I stopped long ago, as a teenager.

While rabbiting on, I study her face. Are there resemblances between us? In that oval face? The grey hair? Maybe, but I am hopelessly unattuned to finding them.

I struggle to find common ground. The course of our lives has run separately for decades. We belong to different generations. We have no shared experience.

As I perceive them, the contrasts reach deeper. I have lived in cities most of my life. She grew up in the country and her family home is by the edge of a bog in central Ireland. My outlook is (for want of a better word) liberal. Olive, despite her life experience, the fact that she was presumably forced to give up a baby, impresses me as a deeply pious woman devoted to the Catholic Church.

We do have some things in common. We both come from modest backgrounds, something Olive notes approvingly. And we are both quiet people, even on this special day.

We soon run out of things to say. I will the minutes to pass, for the experience to be over. In under an hour it is. She places a brown handbag on her lap to signal an end to our talk, and sighs.

'I suppose you'd better get on the road. If you leave now, you might beat the evening traffic.'

It is early still, but I am happy for the invitation to go. We finish up our drinks (tea for her, sparkling water for me), head out onto the sunny street and part company outside the ground-floor entrance to the apartment where she is staying during the week while working locally. After another awkward hug, one that lasts a little longer than the first, I walk back to my car, dazed, not sure what to think.

Not for the first time in my life, I have the sense of important events happening in front of me, rather than to me. I have ticked the box. I have tried to assuage any guilt Olive might have felt. But have I really connected with my birth mother? Should I have been more emotional? Should she? And now that the meeting has taken place, is that it?

26

Some reunions between adopted children and their birth mothers work out fine. Others are disastrous. Mine was underwhelming.

Initial meetings often go well, buoyed up by the release of pent-up emotions and the element of curiosity. Subsequently, I had been warned, a sense of anti-climax can set in, as both parent and child wrestle with the 'what now?' of their new relationship.

Most often, contact between adoptees and birth mothers ends after a single meeting, and no relationship develops, my adoption agency used to claim. I suspect this was said to discourage adoptees from tracing their birth mothers. Still, the challenge of building a relationship between two people whose lives have run entirely separate courses over decades cannot be underestimated.

After our first encounter, Olive and I settled into a low-key acquaintanceship. 'I'm sure that you are an angry young man in some ways. It wasn't so nice being an only child and then it must have been awful for you when your father died quite suddenly,' she told me, in a letter sent days after we met. Olive was a straight talker, I could see.

She did say she was impressed by me and suggested I meet the other members of her family. They had known of my existence for some time.

I had resolved that Mam must know nothing about my contact with my birth mother. Neither could anyone else on her side of the family be told – not her sister or my closest cousins. Because I lived in fear that she might find out, I kept almost all my friends in the dark. It was just too great a risk to take; I could not be confident one of them wouldn't blurt it out accidentally one day.

Little changed for me. Olive was in my life now, but hardly featured in my thoughts. I called into her home, just outside a low-key rural village a few times a year, and met her husband, four children and relatives. Occasionally, when I was in the area for work, I dropped in unannounced. At times, months would go by with no contact, until guilt got the better of me and I paid her a visit. We did meet a few times in Dublin, but I was uncomfortable with these encounters in public places, constantly scanning the room in case someone I knew appeared.

I think we both shied away from deepening our relationship too quickly. She rightly understood that there were limits beyond which she could not stray, given that my adoptive mother was still alive. I had sufficiently 'othered' my birth mother for so much of my life that I found it easy enough to put her out of my mind.

I remember one typical visit to her rural home: the brief awkward hug at the door; the plates of ham and cheese sandwiches she had prepared, though I'd said I wouldn't be hungry; the long silences when neither of us could rise to lively chat; my relief when others arrived, stoking up the conversation and masking my failure to bond with my birth mother.

Olive had little to say when others were around to do the talking. She preferred to busy herself making tea and sandwiches, rather than talk about the past. I did begin to develop a friendship with her adult children, especially her two daughters, who were closer to me in age and outlook.

She continued to write me the odd letter on her favoured Basildon Bond paper, short missives to update me on family news or to inform me that I was in her prayers. Postcards also arrived from Knock and other religious shrines. I had to look up some of the abbreviations she used, which came from another era – TG meant 'thank God' and DV '*Deo volente*/God willing'. The content was often bland, but I noticed she didn't shy away from making judgements and falling back on the rigid strain of religion that had lost me to her decades earlier. When I got married, she wrote to express her disappointment that the wedding hadn't taken place in a church.

In my replies, I filled her in on my life, not shying away from references to 'Mam' and 'my mother'. Again, I sought to allay any guilt that she might have had about relinquishing me for adoption, but I didn't sense any feelings of remorse on her part.

Or maybe it was that she was so understated that she found it hard to express emotions.

I had conceived of my meeting with Olive as a first step of discovery about my origins. Frustratingly, it was hard to find the right time to raise this sensitive topic. When I did, she was loath to talk about it. She closed down any further conversation about my father, beyond repeating that he was a garda.

'They were different times,' she told me. 'That's just the way things were. You had to go along with it.'

I took a relaxed approach, figuring she would open up more in time. But she never did.

27

In my dreams, my accident is a yellow-eyed demon wrapping long tentacles around me, poking for weaknesses. Nine months on from my mountain fall, the demon and its grasp is receding, but still it oozes towards me in unexpected ways. When I experience gastro-intestinal problems, investigations show they are due to a hernia I developed during the fall. Another complication to manage, though the symptoms are mild.

In my head, the recriminations kick in. Was my fall an accident, just one of those things that happens to people? Or was it somehow destined to occur, given my history?

After all, the fall on Zugspitze was not my first mountain mishap. Once, while climbing with a friend in the French Alps, I was struck by lightning. We found ourselves sprawled on the ground, three or four metres away, surprised but unharmed. We were young and chuckled at our good luck, although, as the years went by, I would see a couple of friends killed by these freak events.

Lightning doesn't strike twice, they say, but on another occasion I was part of a group climbing snow-encrusted cliffs on Ben Nevis's north face when a sudden storm forced us to take shelter for the night. This involved digging holes in the snow and ice large enough to take two of us at a time in our bivouac bags.

When morning came, the storm was still raging. Despite the high winds, the mountain remained cloaked in thick fog. Our food and drink was all but gone. There was nothing for it but to call mountain rescue. By the time it arrived by foot five hours later, we were hypothermic. It took 300 metres of abseiling before we reached the bottom of the mountain, and safety.

Our rescue made the news back in Ireland, but thankfully we weren't identified. Mam never learned of the danger I had faced. I certainly wasn't going to tell her about it.

Work had also became more hazardous. Much of my reporting career has been spent in quiet rooms, recording the remarks of politicians, judges, lawyers, doctors and the like, or sitting in front of a computer monitor. But I have also worked in more unpredictable environments, at home and abroad.

The first time I heard gunfire, I was travelling with an Irish aid worker in eastern Zaire shortly after the Rwandan genocide. Armed groups were fighting proxy wars across the region. The noise sounded comical at first, like the pop of a toy gun. In my naïveté, I didn't realise the threat we were facing.

My travelling companion, a seasoned Trócaire staffer, knew better. On hearing the shots, she slammed on the brakes of her jeep, turning it sideways and bringing it to a sudden halt. The two of us crept out of the passenger door and hid behind the wheelbase until the shooting stopped. Two people died that day in the attack by random insurgents.

In 2004, I covered an outbreak of violence at a Traveller camp in Finglas in north Dublin. Though the situation was clearly volatile, I strode into the camp, past the garda checkpoint, in search of interviewees. A rangy youth confronted me, demanding my mobile phone. When I refused to hand it over, he punched me in the face. The blow drew blood and knocked my glasses to the ground. I ran for my life, pursued by an angry dog. Maybe the youth also gave chase, I didn't turn to look. I was blind anyway without my glasses. I made it back to the safety of the checkpoint without either youth or dog catching me.

My biggest brush with danger occurred in 2000 when I was working as development correspondent for *The Irish Times*, often reporting from disaster zones. I was covering devastating flooding in Mozambique, where rising river waters had killed over 800 people. On the last night, I found myself without anywhere to stay in the capital, Maputo. Staff from the aid agency Concern helpfully offered to put me up.

I awoke that night in a stiflingly hot room to the sound of strangers moving about my bedroom. There seemed to be three of them – all men – knocking over chairs, arguing in a language I did not understand.

Two of the men had knives, and the third carried what

looked like a small gun. One grabbed my shoulder and forced me around on the bed, shoving my head down into the pillow.

I closed my eyes and awaited my fate. And started to count, breathing heavily into the mattress. One-two-three-four; a small eternity. My hands were gripped from behind and bound together with a cable tie. Five-six-seven-eight. The man moved down to my ankles and bound them too.

My body stiffened as the racket continued. The men were bickering among themselves, the noise level rising. Were they arguing over what to do with me?

I heard a door flung open, and then a cry from one of the other rooms. Muffled talk, then silence. Had someone been attacked? Would I be next?

But when the men returned to my room, they were calmer. They had neutralised any threat from the occupants of the house. I heard scuffling noises behind me, the sound of booty being gathered.

Very quickly they were gone. The worst was over. But I was unable to free myself. I lay trussed up on the sweaty mattress for an age. Morning broke before help came and we were cut loose. Thankfully, despite my worst imaginings, no-one was hurt.

The gang had missed my passport, or hadn't bothered taking it. I was able to fly home the next day as originally scheduled, my pockets empty. I convinced myself that I was fine, declined offers of counselling and carried on as if nothing had happened.

Back in Ireland after the robbery, everything appeared to be okay with me. But a year later, when I was due to return to Africa for the first time after the incident, I noticed a loss of nerve. Flying south, I felt uncharacteristically jumpy. My destination this time was Nigeria, the most populous country in Africa. I knew no-one there.

Fortunately, an 'Irish mafia' exists everywhere. Generous missionaries in Lagos offered to put me up. Walking around the slums of the city with these humble men, I stuck close by their side until I felt my confidence return. The trip passed safely, but I wasn't the same gung-ho person I had been before.

Thinking about these incidents now in the aftermath of an event that almost did end my life, I wondered about their frequency. I had grown overly familiar with risk, and often seemed blasé in the face of danger. On the night we were stuck in the snow near the top of Ben Nevis, one of my fellow climbers 'lost it' and started keening for his young children, yet I remained desensitised to the threat we were facing.

It wasn't just that I didn't have children at the time. I didn't have blood relatives of any kind; well, they were out there, presumably, but I didn't know anything about them. That left me feeling strangely detached from mankind, alone in the crowd.

Because I wasn't physically harmed in these incidents, I began to think I was indestructible, which possibly put me even more in harm's way. But I had been affected, I could see now. These shocks had had a profound, if hidden, impact on my wellbeing, one I was only beginning to understand. I was overdue a reckoning with my past, even before I ran out of luck on Zugspitze.

28

It is said that adopted people struggle to make lasting attachments. We are said to need constant reassurance, to fear losing what connections we do have.

I am the worst person to judge how my complex collage of traits and defining characteristics fits the adopted stereotype. There are definitely challenging aspects to my character. Cranky, irascible, impatient, arrogant. I'll argue the toss over minor points until I'm half dead, then recant in the morning. I can have difficulty reading the room, preferring clean logic over messy emotion. The intensity with which I'll debate an issue is often in inverse proportion to its importance.

I can feel like a misfit, though I am not one. A loner too, when, patently, I am not alone. Somehow, I seem to have been spared many of the problematic traits commonly ascribed to adopted people. Early in primary school, good people sought me out, claiming me as their friend. I didn't know why I was deemed worthy, but it certainly helped my confidence.

I added more friendships in later years in school and college.

The special people I met along life's way played a crucial part in drawing me closer to the rest of mankind. They lured me away from the perils of isolation, driven by my experience as an only child growing up with a profound sense of difference.

My parents, typical of their generation, were modest, undemonstrative people. 'Every day of his life, your father turned away from me to put on his pyjamas,' a reflective Mam told me once, near the end of her life. Yet they gave me enough love to feel wanted.

They were poor at expressing or showing affection, but it was there all the same. It revealed itself in the ridiculous pride Mam exuded when talking to others about 'my Paul', which caused friends and family to smile. It was there in the quiet time Dad and I spent on projects together and the calm humility he showed me. It was there in the many material sacrifices they made for me.

In contrast to my strait-laced family, the friends I made in college were abundant huggers and kissers, and though their tactility felt strange to me initially, I got used to close contact and learned to reciprocate. And while others saw me as unemotional, under that hard shell beat a heart as soft as butter. Responding to petty injustices or sentimental storylines, my tears flowed freely, just as they had all those years before when I read the book about the lion who died before his time.

Clichéd or no, for many years I believed I, like other adoptees, would struggle to form lasting relationships. I was shy with girls initially, and the atmosphere at home hardly helped. When romance came my way, I tended to engage for a while, then move on. Others were forming long-term relationships and getting married, but this wasn't for me. Not getting stuck was my schtick. In the back of my mind lay thoughts of the chaotic circumstances in which I'd arrived in the world. I was anxious that history would not repeat itself.

So I spent my thirties in a form of extended boyhood. I ran marathons, scaled peaks in the Alps and cycled across Europe. I wasn't in any way exceptional at these endeavours but I had an unremitting restlessness that had to be assuaged. Pushing myself to my physical limits gave me meaning. Striving to achieve distracted me from existential conundrums closer to home. I placed little value on my own safety.

At the same time, my career was developing. After a spell as education correspondent with *The Irish Times*, I was assigned to write stories from the developing world, mostly Africa. In these years, I criss-crossed the world on long-haul flights, covering successive natural and man-made disasters – conflict, famine, flooding and disease among them. I had a front row seat for the world's misery.

But I wasn't away all the time. It was through work that I met the woman who was to become my partner in life. Dee and I crossed paths when we were both working for *The Irish Times* at the inauguration of Mary McAleese as Irish president in November 1997. As the newly elected president talked on the theme of building bridges, we made our acquaintance in the grand surroundings of St Patrick's Hall in Dublin Castle.

Six months later, we met again at a ball, and started going out together. Opposites attracted in our relationship to create a complementary union. From the start, I'd never felt so thoroughly understood. The penultimate barrier to me feeling a normal, well-adjusted human being was swept away; there was never any doubt in my mind that we would spend our lives together. Fortunately, Dee felt the same way.

In the past, I had been just as dubious about fatherhood as I was about lasting attachments. With no small nephews or nieces of my own, children were foreign to me. Given my birth father's absence from my life, I was afraid I might repeat that pattern. I would not have children, I resolved, because of the mess that was made of my conception and the grief it must have caused so many people.

I summoned the great writers in support of my stance. Hadn't Philip Larkin warned how 'Man hands on misery to man' by having children? And what about Cyril Connolly's quip about the 'pram in the hall' being the 'enemy of good art'?

In hindsight, these quotes were cheap cover for insecurities I had picked up along the way. My taboo against fatherhood dissolved quickly enough once I revised my thinking and the stars aligned.

As part of my volte-face, and rejecting Larkin's advice, I doubled down on having children. I would atone for the way I came into the world by providing *my* children with a settled, stable upbringing. I would be an active father, closely involved with them. And I would have multiple children so they could grow up with the sisters or brothers I had often wished for. There would be no only child in my family, if I could help it.

Dee and I married in 2003 and she became pregnant the following year. With change in the air, part of me wanted to push myself even harder before I became a father, while another part was already making adjustments.

Before the baby was due, I went on a work assignment to the Democratic Republic of the Congo. On the way back, waiting in the airport in Kinshasa, I noticed a small shop called Bobo's. Bobo – wasn't that the nickname we had given Dee's bump, soon to be our first child? I just had to take a picture.

Bad idea – and I could feel it the moment the camera lens clicked. Do not take photos when surrounded by armed soldiers, especially in an airport when they have nothing to do except shake down passing travellers.

Instantly, a man in military fatigues bore down upon me. I had broken the ordinance forbidding the taking of photographs in military zones. Didn't I know this was a crime punishable by long imprisonment?

I could smell the beer off his breath as he demanded my passport. Explaining why I had taken the photo might get lost in translation, so I just said I was sorry.

Half a dozen soldiers surrounded me, shouting in my face. They grabbed my bag and started to rifle through it. Camera, passport, said one. Another soldier, his dead eyes bloodshot and weeping, pointed a gun at me. This time, I readily offered up my passport.

Beery Breath whipped it out of my hand. 'Come with me,' he barked. 'We must go to the barracks.'

I tried to resist but his friends jostled me along. By now, I was sweating like a drugs mule. Despairingly, I looked over at the line of passengers boarding the aeroplane, all of them with their heads down. What a mess, of my own making. Visions of months spent languishing in a Congolese dungeon hovered before me. Rats. Cockroaches. Mosquitoes. God knows what else. And all while my first child was due back in Ireland.

My phone was dead. I couldn't contact anyone. There was only one thing for it, and no time to lose. Digging my hand into a pocket, I fished out a $50 bill. I had the soldier's attention now but he didn't move. I pulled out another $50 and squashed the two notes into his chest. He grabbed the money with his fist and pocketed it instantly. Walking away, he clicked his fingers. My passport rematerialised from the scrum of soldiers and was thrown in my direction. The group sauntered off, laughing.

Dumbstruck – did that *really* just happen? – I sped off to board the plane. I could not get out of the country fast enough. At least I had the photos of Bobo's to show to Dee.

That same summer, I travelled back to Switzerland to fulfil a long-held ambition to climb the Matterhorn. The weather was unstable and there was heavy snow on the mountain, so I was forced to kick my heels in Zermatt until it improved.

I waited and waited and still the skies refused to clear. All the time, the feeling grew in me that I no longer belonged there, not when my wife was at home, pregnant with our first child. And, by extension, that I no longer belonged on the mountain, given the risks involved. I changed my flight and came home early. The Matterhorn could wait for another day, I told myself.

Christmas Day, and a light snow is falling as we leave the maternity hospital. Stopping briefly to ask a nurse to snap us before the tree, all tinsel and baubles, a five-pointed star on top. Exhausted mother on one side, exhausted father on the other. Between them, a tiny milk-scented bundle in a car seat – our newborn daughter, born three weeks late, after an arduous delivery.

Ella had threatened to upend Christmas completely by refusing to arrive, but eventually had the good grace to be born on the winter solstice, that moment when the days stop shortening and the world can start thinking again of better, brighter days. Now it is her turn to sleep, as her parents gather up their things and head out into the wintry streets outside.

Father. Parent. How strange it feels to attach these words to my name. My daughter, flesh of my flesh. The birth of a child a wondrous event for anyone, but especially for someone not used to having blood relatives. This definitely feels like a new phase of my life.

Long before the contractions started coming, Dee and I had promised Mam that we would call up on Christmas Day. All we want to do is collapse into bed and fuss over our new daughter, but our first stop has to be Marian Grove.

Mam, as usual at this time of year, has put on a big spread. As the daughter of a butcher, she always prided herself on her festive dinners. This year is no exception, despite the oxygen cannula she wears now by day as well as at night. The table in the front room groans with food, enough to feed a large family. None of us has any appetite – apart from Ella.

Mam has lived long enough to hold a grandchild in her arms. At eighty-five and hanging on to life by a thread, she is beyond physically caring for small babies. Still, she musters a game smile for a photo with my baby daughter. A grandmother at last! And although physically frail, she is quick to issue parenting advice. Trouble is, her behavioural tips have more relevance to a toddler than to a freshly minted baby – she is put out that Ella is not babbling to her. But then I remember she missed out on the newborn stage with me the first time around. She is keen to dispense her parental wisdom because, she knows, soon it will be too late.

Though I had embraced fatherhood, I thought I might struggle with the reality of it over the first few years of Ella's life, until she was old enough to talk and interact with people. Before this, I had hardly changed a nappy.

To my surprise, though, I loved caring for a small baby. I was smitten by my daughter: by her fragility; the way she smelled (most of the time); the impossible smoothness of her skin. I loved how quickly she changed every week in those early years, and was gratified to learn that communication with a child gets established long before the actual words arrive. It all felt like the natural way of the world.

I thought: if I'm enjoying this, how might my father have felt if he had been around for me? In this way, having my own children became a prompt for researching my past.

29

Mam lay exhausted on her hospital bed, battling to draw each breath. Years of repeated chest infections were finally taking their toll, the times between hospital admissions getting shorter as her chronic obstructive pulmonary disease (COPD) got worse.

This hospital stay was different. There were no more requests for the evening paper or a few chips from the local greasy-spoon café. She had no further strength to rail against the world.

By 2005, the fight had finally gone out of her; the anger too. Curiously, I found this more distressing than the prospect of losing her. One day, a patient died on the other side of the thin curtain separating her bed from the others in the ward. She didn't even notice. I held her hand and talked into the ether, not knowing or caring whether she was hearing me or not. I talked for the sake of talking, about this and that. Most of all, I told her I loved her, because those words were never used often enough when I was growing up, or were deployed too late, after hurt had been inflicted. I cried. Many of those tears were for myself.

I was at work when the final call came from the hospital. She was nearing the end. I willed the tram to move faster as it snaked out of the city and up towards Tallaght Hospital and the hills beyond. Mam was asleep when I arrived, but apparently still alive. There was nothing to do but hold her hand again and wonder at how tiny she had become. Skin, loose on bone; her as fragile as one of the nestlings she used to rescue from the neighbourhood cats. She lasted an hour or so, then slipped away.

I spoke at Mam's funeral in the same church where my parents had attended Mass every Sunday, where I had made my Communion and sung in the choir, and where Dad's funeral had been held twenty years earlier.

'Mam was a woman of many parts; she was also a woman *from* many parts,' I told the mourners – the Liberties, Harold's Cross, Donegal, Argentina. Some of these links were real; others less so.

Like every dutiful son, I paid tribute to her great energy and drive. How Christmas started months earlier each year with the baking of cakes and the boiling of puddings, in greater number than the three of us would ever need. How no effort was spared in the creation of a Christmas Day dinner, from the ham basted in front of the fire the evening before to the outsize turkey that barely fitted in the oven and would have fed the entire road, never mind our little family.

I talked of my parents' close relationship, the pair of them partners in everything. 'Hospital visits, gardening, spoiling the child. Dad wore the overalls, but she definitely wore the trousers,' I said, drawing a knowing laugh from those who knew them.

She was, I told the mourners, 'one of the most remarkable women I have ever known'. I meant that.

Perhaps I was only now coming to terms with my loss: 'From the time she and Patrick took me into their home at the age of two-and-a-half, to 6.15 p.m. last Wednesday, she has dominated my life. For the most part, for the better – much of what I am today, I have my mother to thank for.

'She taught me to strive for myself, and for her too, and I did. She taught me basic values of decency, honesty, neighbourliness and fair play. "There is a right way of doing something, and there is a wrong way," she would say, leaving me in no doubt as to which course I should follow.

'We didn't always see eye to eye,' I admitted. But on this point, I deflected, keeping things light: 'Mam told me never to talk about religion or politics, and so I became a journalist and got paid for *writing* about religion and politics.'

I paid tribute to her good works – visiting the sick, helping to deliver neighbours' babies at home back in the old days, Christmas and Sunday dinners for the next-door neighbour. Then it was all over. I buried her beside Dad in their plot on the side of a mountain, the cemetery no less bleak than it was when he died twenty years earlier. After giving mourners tea and sandwiches in a local pub, I went home with Dee to mind the baby.

Mam, I reflected, had a unique and endearing way of interacting with people. She talked to anyone, young or old, whether they wished to engage in conversation or not. In the abstract, she could be hostile, suspicious, misogynistic; when talking to someone, she was unfailingly polite and helpful. She was at her funniest when putting on airs, often mangling the English language, but she could laugh at herself too. And she could cook a mean Christmas dinner.

My parents were both dead now, and the home where I grew up lay empty. In mid-life, I had become an orphan. Or had I, given that I had another mother kept under wraps and another father out there somewhere?

Mam's importance in my life had shrunk with time, just as she had diminished physically. I had long ceased to regard her as a threat to my equilibrium, though we could still cross swords on occasion. Her death had less of an impact on me than if it had occurred twenty years earlier. Besides, I was busy at home.

Her instructions to me continued from the grave. Amid a sheaf of financial documents, I found this directive, signed by her and Dad, although he was long dead at the time it was written: *You don't let anyone tell you what to do.*

In sorting out her affairs, I located the old Dairy Box chocolate carton containing information about my adoption. I couldn't recall having seen it before. Or maybe I had, and then forgotten about it. I decided to do nothing with it for now, aside from stowing it in the attic.

There it was to remain for years, contents unviewed, while I got on with the sleep-deprived helter-skelter of life as a new father and a busy reporter.

30

The text comes in from a friend first thing on a Sunday morning.

Sorry!

Followed immediately by a second message.

I was out of order.

Damn, he got there first.

No, I'm sorry, I replied. I was out of order. And I started it.

A dull sense of guilt hanging over me as I continue to clean up after the previous night's dinner. What was it exactly that I started?

It was a great night anyway.

Generous of him, but was it? Dipping my hands into the sudsy water, I tried to replay what happened. The party had started well, my friend as witty as ever, role-playing for laughs like a born comedian. Everyone around the table in great form, joining in the chat. Someone cracked a joke about politicians, prompting a few one-liners about the state of the country.

And then me, bringing an edge to things. Restless, exhausted. Wanting to get up and move around, but moving only one muscle – the one lifting my wine glass. Starting an argument to stay with it.

'So, what's your point?' A debating tactic, loudly delivered, sucking the lightness out of the room. 'What exactly is your point?'

My voice rising and my friend's rising in response, the others around the table falling silent. The two of us shouting in each other's face, gesturing, professing mock astonishment – 'You can't be serious!' – me digging ever deeper into a maze of argumentation, unable to find a way out.

Wiser heads prevailing, switching the subject, telling us to park our outrage. Me, the blood still flush in my cheeks, stalking out of the room. What have I done?

And what exactly *was* my point? It won't come back to me now as I dry my hands on the towel, trying to excavate the fuzz of my mind. What exactly was going on with me?

By the late-2000s I was living my busiest life, juggling work and parenthood. Coping with the loss of Mary and keeping Olive and consideration of my adoption at a distance, I carried on as though everything was normal. It was anything but, and about to become extraordinarily difficult.

Looking back on the years that followed my fortieth birthday, it is striking how quickly things went awry. But the seeds of my undoing were planted long before.

My troubles arrived serially rather than landing at the same time, which made them easier to deflect. Cumulatively, though, they set me up for further reverses before I was forced finally to confront the unanswered questions about my past.

Dee and I had been blessed in the formation of a family up to that point, given that I'd started so late. Our first child was born when I was forty-one, a second daughter came along nineteen months later and a third a busy two and a half years after that. Three beautiful girls: Ella, then Rosa and Tana; as easy as 1-2-3. We were steeped.

And then – trouble. We loved having children and were happy to have more. I was enjoying fatherhood much more than I had dared hope. Here I was, an only child and an adopted one too, who had never before experienced blood ties, now blessed with three young daughters of my own.

We were not insouciant about the risks facing older parents, but, after consideration, we opted to go for another child. Whatever the outcome, we knew we would welcome him or her into the world. Just as before, Dee was pregnant quickly, to our absolute delight. We wondered how we would fit the new addition into our now packed house, and whether a boy or a girl was on the way.

One Saturday morning, I was awoken by Dee. She was in pain, cramping and bleeding. We rushed to the same maternity hospital where the girls had been delivered. Staff confirmed what we already knew, that we had lost the baby.

It was a missed miscarriage, at fourteen weeks. Our child most likely died weeks earlier. We had remained in the dark until nature decided to let us know what was really happening.

I have friends who have lost full-term babies; I cannot imagine the levels of grief they experienced. Our loss occurred much earlier, but the miscarriage still hit us hard. Our grief remained private, because we hadn't told people about the pregnancy. Someone precious we never got the chance to know was gone from our lives. We lost the sense of invincibility about our ability to conceive children we had enjoyed up to then.

After a time, though, we were ready to try again. The doctors were not able to say why the miscarriage had occurred. It was, apparently, just one of those things.

Worse was to come. Dee got pregnant again, then miscarried again. And again. And yet again. How could it have come to this?

It is hard to express the sense of loss you experience with a miscarriage. It is not as though I knew any of these tiny beings who expired while still in the womb. Yet their presence hung about me, ghost-like, for so long, joining all the other presences dimly imagined from my early life. It wasn't fair that they were denied a shot at life through some medical quirk.

Inevitably, we grew more nervous with each successive failed pregnancy. We hugged our daughters ever more closely, acutely conscious of what precious gifts they were.

Our goal each time was to get through the first trimester, yet we could not manage this. With our biological clocks ticking away, the odds of having another child were increasingly stacked against us. We weren't interested in assisted reproduction techniques, and spurned the battery of tests suggested by the medical experts. What would be would be.

Though demoralised and exhausted, we decided to throw the dice one more time. Our expectations were at rock bottom. Nothing happened. We prepared to move on, mentally. It wasn't to be.

It was a time for new beginnings. Dee mentioned taking up tennis again, a game she hadn't played since her schooldays. I resolved to surprise her with membership of a local club as a Christmas present. The business of getting the application approved by the committee proved time-consuming. Finally, one night in mid-December, I picked up the signed membership card on the way home from work. Santa could look after the kids, but now I had my own present-giving sorted for Christmas Day.

Dee was on the couch when I arrived home.

'I've got some news.'

I hardly had time to take off my coat.

'I'm pregnant.'

'Oh? Oh!'

Of course I was elated but after all the disappointment, I must have looked confused. I explained about the tennis plan. As we hugged, she said, 'Let's try and get through the next few weeks with this. See how we get on.'

Luca came along the following year to complete our family. I could not have been happier. Here I was, blessed with a loving relationship and four beautiful children, surrounded by a wide circle of friends. Fit and healthy, I was running several marathons a year, had crossed the Alps by bike and competed in Ironman triathlons. What could go wrong?

31

Experts say a lack of resilience – an ability to bounce back after difficult life episodes – affects many adopted people and others who have suffered adverse childhood experiences. We have missed out on the close bonds and loving care most people take for granted in their early years, which can make us brittle. Uncertain of our place in the world, we may lack the normal ability to recover from the traumas that occur later in life.

Resilience levels can improve where an adopted child is provided with stable and supportive care, but in my case this took years to put in place.

My resilience cracked shortly after our fourth child was born in 2013. The straw that broke the camel's back was a controversy over an article I had written. A hazard of the profession and, in the past, something I would have worn lightly. Coming just weeks after Luca's birth, a combination of chronic stress and tiredness was also at play. And there was more.

The fuss at work died down, as it always does, but my confidence was severely dented. I realised how fragile I was feeling.

Luckily, I had already booked a period of unpaid leave, and it couldn't have come at a better time. We had planned to take the children on an adventure. Taking the girls out of school for a year, we threw Luca's babygros into a suitcase. One rainy November morning, the family flew out of Dublin, bound for Central America.

For six months, we lived a nomadic life in Nicaragua and Costa Rica, moving from one rented house to another as the mood took us. The girls attended local schools as we perfected the art of baby dandling while learning Spanish under the equatorial sun. I had time to think.

It was the strangest of times. I was still in a daze, yet we had landed on our feet. The family slotted happily into the easy pace of life of Granada, an old colonial outpost in Nicaragua, one of the most off-the-grid countries in the world. As well as the locals, the town was home to a surreal collection of blow-ins – former IRA members, swindlers, enterprising Irish mavericks, ageing US army veterans blowing their welfare cheques on cheap beer.

Notwithstanding the colourful cast of local characters, there was plenty of time to mull over what had happened. What had provoked my collapse? I had experienced a great deal of stress, but was there something else that contributed to my reaction? If I didn't know the answer to this question, wasn't it time to find out? If Olive wouldn't tell me about the past, wouldn't I have to find it out myself?

We returned to Ireland from Central America refreshed and rejuvenated. I fished out the box of personal documents from under the bed. It contained the usual jumble of mementos and oddments: official documents, a handful of picture albums, copies of old newspapers.

All that related to my adoption fitted in a thin manila envelope: a few letters from the adoption agency to my parents; my baptism cert; a claim form for children's allowance. It wasn't a lot to start with, but I was determined now to make progress. I made an application to the Catholic Protection and Rescue Society of Ireland (CPRSI) for more information.

In the box, I came across a leaflet issued by the CPRSI in the 1960s that my parents must have relied upon for guidance. *Telling the Child* stressed the responsibility of parents to rear their adopted child in the knowledge that he or she was adopted, and to tell them about this fact as early as possible. When the child asked about his or her 'real parents', the leaflet advised parents to reply: 'We don't know; we never knew; we never wanted to know, as all we wanted was you.'

So not only were parents told not to provide any information to their adopted children – they wouldn't generally have been provided with the details – but they were also given tips on shutting down any conversation about birth parents.

Within weeks of returning, a fresh scandal erupted at home. In County Galway, a local historian established that almost 800 children had died at the Bon Secours mother and baby home in Tuam and concluded that many were buried in unmarked graves on the site.

Over many years, Catherine Corless had assembled the death certificates of the children who were resident in the home, but she could find few burial records. The children might have been deposited over decades in an area of the site that once housed the home's septic tanks, her research suggested. The site was widely described by media and commentators as a 'mass grave'.

The resulting furore shone a light on the twilight world of mother and baby homes across the state. Between the 1920s and 1990s, about 56,000 women and girls passed through these homes. More than 60,000 children were born in them.

Abandoned by their families and stigmatised by society, these unmarried mothers suffered abuse, neglect and mistreatment. Many of the children were adopted but up to 9,000 died in the homes, in many cases due to poor conditions, inadequate medical care or malnutrition.

The Tuam scandal echoed around the world. Under pressure to act, the government set up a commission of investigation into the homes. Suddenly, the voices of birth mothers and adopted people were being heard more clearly than before.

I responded to this news as I had to every new development over the years: outwardly sceptical while questioning within. Could I have spent time in a mother and baby home? The thought had never crossed my mind and there was nothing in the information I had to suggest this. The notion seemed far-fetched.

Perhaps because I was now a father myself, I developed a greater interest in my birth father. Men were curiously absent from the debate then raging over mother and baby homes, in which the Catholic Church and the state were taking most of the flak. To me, this amounted to letting the men in ill-fated extra-marital unions off the hook. Where was my own father when I was born? And why was Olive so reluctant to talk about him?

32

Winter sunlight streams through the windows. Some day, I promise myself, I'll give them a good clean, if I ever get time. The street outside is quiet in the dip between Christmas and New Year but in our front room a small child is bustling about with no regard for the early hour of the day, as 2015 moves towards a close.

My son is half-running, half-staggering around the room, chortling at me as he recites his favourite nursery rhymes. The words come out slow, and then fast. Many are spoken clearly, others blur into a mush of mumble. He bluffs the lines he doesn't know:

Jack and Jill went up the hill and fetch pail of water
Jack fell down broke his crown
Jill come tumbling after

He freezes for a moment, tugs at his pyjamas with a mischievous grin, then starts whirling around again:

Up Jack got, and home trot,
As fast as he ehhhh,
To ehhh who ehh

With a flourish of waving hands, the little boy delivers his finale:

Vinega and bwown pape-eh!

He stops theatrically, a gleeful smile still fixed on his face, but only for an instant.

'I want a playdate!'

All earnestness and beseeching, the straw licks of his hair caught now in pale beams of sunlight. So endearing, so lovable, so tiny and yet so complete. The intense pain of filial love, so strong I have to look away.

'A playdate? At this time of the morning?'

'I want a playdate!'

A small stamp of the foot, a furrowing of his brow.

'Maybe later.'

'But I want a playdate!'

Feigned anger. But this could go round in circles. Distraction is needed.

'Tell me now, what's your name?'

'Luca!'

'Luca what?'

'Luca Cullen.'

'And how old is Luca?'

'Two. I two years, four months.' Six fingers in the air.

'Two years and four months. That's a fine age. And when is your birthday?'

'Six months.' Six fingers up again, good boy.

'In six months. When is that?'

'July.'

'And when in July?'

'Sunday!'

'Okay. What would you like on your birthday?'

A sly, sideways look.

'Sweeties!'

'What else?'

'Marshmallows!'

'What else?'

'Biscuits?'

Need to change the subject. 'Erm, do you like trucks, lorries?'

'Sugar! Cereal! Porridge!'

'Never mind that. What do you see every morning?'

'Wake up.'

'Yes, but after you get up and go out, what do you see? On the road, when you're going to nursery?'

'Digger. Dig hole!'

But he has lost interest in this line of chat. Another spin, another rhyme:

Little Miss Muffet
Sat on a tuffet
Eating her curds away
'Long came a spider …

I have stopped listening. Somewhere inside me a light has come on. This small being in front of me, this fully formed little boy, with words and attitudes and arguments and so much joy – this was me. *This was me, once.* Two years and four months – up to that age I was in limbo, neither with my birth mother nor with my adoptive parents. No birth father present, or even on the horizon. I was a living, breathing, rounded mini-human capable of movement, speech and humour – and yet, even today, I know nothing about where I was or how I was at this time.

Luca kicking a ball. Luca stabbing at the piano with two fingers. Luca picking out colours. Luca charging down the road. *This was me. This was me, at his age.*

Or was it? If a tree falls in the woods and no-one hears it, has it made a sound? My early years – unwitnessed, unrecorded, unremembered – are one big void. That absence has stayed with me all my life, I realise, but I have never felt it so strongly as in this moment of small revelation.

Of course I should have experienced this epiphany before, when we started having children. But it was different with my daughters. Little girls are satellites of Venus; little boys moons of Mars.

There is nothing to compare with the experience of nurturing a first child. Watching each of the three girls grow up was a marvel. But raising Luca is on another level, because I am looking at a mirror of myself. We are joined by our Y chromosomes, and so much more.

Where was I when I was his exact age? Was I adored?

Encouraged? Indulged? Or was I ignored? Chastised? Abused even? Suddenly, I am a torment of fears, full of worry over things I can do nothing about.

Luca has stopped reciting his rhymes. He lays a tiny hand on mine.

'Why sad, Daddy? Why sad?'

For most people, families serve as a looking-glass. They only have to look at their siblings, children or parents to see a reflection of their own traits. Adoptees, with no genetic link to the families in which they grow up, have no such mirror. The normal feedback loop that contributes to the development of character is absent.

Throughout my life, my default was to regard people as being 'other' or 'different' from me. I was never in the habit of looking out for features, or even psychological traits, I might have in common with others. As a new father, though, I found myself holding my own kin for the first time, tiny humans related to me by the precious ties of blood and genetics. Realising there was a little bit of me in my daughters' blue eyes or my son's fair hair made me keen to find out about the elements of my make-up.

But it was more specific than that. The epiphany I had when Luca was playing in the front room brought home a truth I hadn't understood up to that point. Those missing first years of my life were so important; I needed to find out more.

33

'Look, what is it you want to know?'

Ten minutes into my meeting with the social worker, and it was clear from her exasperated tone that things were not going well. The person across the desk at the CPRSI had changed, my old social worker having retired, but the emphasis on secrecy was the same.

'I'd like full access to my file,' I said, my voice rising. 'And you're saying: "You can't have it." Why can't you give it to me? What are your reasons?'

'It's the legislation that's in place at the moment,' the young woman across the table replied. 'We can't release identifying information.'

'You mean the 1952 Adoption Act?' So much time had passed, and yet so little had changed. Here I was in 2017, banging up against the reality so many other adoptees had faced for decades.

'Yes, as an adoption agency, all we can release is non-identifying information about other persons. We can give you factual information about yourself that is on the records, but we can't provide addresses or names of birth parents without their permission.'

Some months before, the agency had sent me a summary of my file. Just thirteen pages, but it did contain some new information. I learned exactly where I was born – in a hospital in north London. The document also mentioned where I was baptised – *in a mother and baby home*. The home was not named, and it was not in Ireland, but in London.

This was news to me. The certificate I had always possessed gave the place of my baptism as a church in London.

Though not stated explicitly, it was clear that I had once lived in this mother and baby home.

Never for a moment before this had I thought the scandal around these homes had anything to do with me personally. Now I was learning that I had spent my first weeks of life in one.

There was more. The day after my arrival in Ireland at the age of almost five months, I was placed in foster care. Again there were no details, but I remained in some form of foster care for more than two years.

It was a lot to take in. But the document was full of gaps. It didn't contain much else about my early life, and said nothing at all about the period before I was born. There was more about the sums of money demanded of Olive for my care than there was about me; more emphasis on efficient administration than my human needs. I wasn't happy, so I sought a meeting.

Which was how I found myself making my way once more to the South Anne Street offices. Entering through its glossy red door, I waited in the building's dark interior, as nervous as I was on previous occasions. The agency was known now as Cúnamh, the Irish for assistance or help, having rebranded in 1992. I hoped that indicated a willingness to share more information.

'This is a file about me, going back to a time I can't recall because I was so young,' I explained to the social worker; this was becoming a familiar refrain from me. 'It would be very moving for me to see it.'

'Any information about you is there. But about your adoptive parents, say, we can share letters that were sent, but we can't release their adoption assessment.'

'But my parents are dead. This is all so long ago.'

I prodded her this way and that, seeking more information, without any success.

'Well then, how big is my file?'

'Erm, I don't know exactly.'

I told her of my surprise at learning I had spent time in a mother and baby home in London. 'You must have dealt with many cases where women gave birth in London and were in a mother and baby home there?'

'I can really only talk about your own case.'

'So you can't tell me anything? What about my foster mother, for example. Is she still alive?'

'I'm not aware if she is or not.'

Assuming that it was a woman, that is. 'And were other kids placed with her?'

'I don't know, I can't tell you that. I can only talk about your case.'

Our conversation ran in more loops than a crop circle, or so I felt. The social worker's caution about disclosing information verged on the farcical. She referred to my putative birth father only by his first name, Vincent. Yet Olive had given me a full name for him – Vincent Duffy. The social worker knew this and it must, surely, correspond to the name on the file she refused to share with me. But under the marching orders given to her, she had to pretend not to know this.

She did offer to carry out a search for this man but warned that it would take up to nine months. And though she knew I had been to Olive's home, she would say only that my birth mother was from 'Leinster'.

The discussion meandered on for an hour before I wrapped it up. We chatted neutrally about our holiday plans as she let me out, my frustration palpable under a veneer of politeness.

I followed up by letter, demanding to know in writing why the agency would not release my full file. Why couldn't it release information about my adoptive parents, I asked, given that they were both dead.

The social worker stuck to her guns, leaning on legal advice received by the agency years earlier. 'Senior Counsel's opinion at that time was to the effect that the only circumstances in which the release of the full original file could be permitted would be if there was a court order in place directing Cúnamh to do this,' she recited.

Her search for Vincent '—' came to nothing, foundering on the lack of a birth date or home address for him. The door to more information had been prised open a bit; I had learned something from chasing the CPRSI. For now, though, it seemed I was stuck.

Six months later, I had my accident in Germany. Following that life-changing event, seeking answers was no longer just an option; it became an imperative.

34

The development of the brain starts before a child is born. Then, during the first two years of life, it forms over a million neural connections – synapses – *every second*, a pace never repeated. By age two the brain has reached about three-quarters of its adult weight, and by age six, 90 per cent.

And while the brain overproduces synapses in early life, it refines them through a process known as synaptic pruning. Frequently used connections become stronger, while unused ones are lost. In this way, early experiences shape the architecture of the brain.

Even in the first year, babies are alert to specific speech sounds that help them develop language skills. If they are not exposed to these sounds, they may lose the ability to distinguish them. They communicate initially by babbling and copying sounds, and then start to understand familiar words. By twelve months, they may be saying their first words, and by eighteen months, their first sentences.

During my recuperation, I read with voracious interest books on child development and psychology. The first years of a baby's life are critical for overall development, laying down the pathways for future behaviour, learning and wellbeing. It sets the stage for everything that happens later in life. Every aspect of the child's growth is affected, from brain development to the formation of lasting emotional bonds.

Secure attachments provide the base from which children can confidently explore the world, manage emotions and develop healthy coping strategies, I read. In contrast, disruption can have significant emotional and psychological effects.

Researchers distinguish between different forms of stress. Positive stress, in small amounts, can be beneficial for development, helping to build resilience. Toxic stress – when a child experiences strong, frequent or prolonged adversity, without supportive relationships as a buffer – can disrupt brain and organ development and lead to lifelong health issues.

Much of the thinking on babies' attachment to parents and others was developed by British psychotherapist John Bowlby, whose theories emphasise the importance of early emotional bonds between a child and their caregiver. Bowlby proposed that these bonds are vital for survival and emotional development, serving as a foundation for future relationships.

Infants have an innate need to attach to one primary caregiver, Bowlby believed. This relationship is qualitatively different from all others and serves as a template for all future relationships. From the age of just six weeks, babies show a clear preference for their primary caregivers. From six months, they experience separation anxiety when that person leaves.

If an attachment has not developed during a 'critical period' of the first few years of a child's life, then it may well not happen at all, Bowlby posited. Even good mothering was almost useless if delayed after the age of two and a half, he wrote in 1951 – a thoroughly depressing finding, from my point of view. In later work, and in response to new research, he softened this assertion, by proposing an expanded 'sensitive period' of up to five years. During this window, some healthy bonding could still take place; attachments were often insecure, but not impossible.

Despite the challenges I faced, I knew I was capable of secure attachment. But given these research findings, the question I'd spent so long dodging hit me with renewed force. In those first years, after Olive had given me up for adoption, where was I? What care did I receive? And from whom?

My return to work after the accident continues to be a mix of blue skies and cloud. Almost a year on, my strength has returned, despite the demands of juggling home life with work shifts. My body, though, does not want to return to normal. Intermittent pain wells up from deep within me, as damaged bones and nerve endings jar and jangle against each other. I need to pull back from vigorous exercise until I mend further. At home, I take short breaks in bed, where lying horizontally brings some relief.

Physiotherapy helps to get me over the worst flare-ups. I make a half-hearted attempt to access treatment in hospital, but the Irish health service isn't strong on rehab and my injuries aren't severe enough now to demand the attention of hard-pressed specialists. I try an osteopath, who is unable to help. Friends recommend other specialists, from bone setters to sacro-cranial therapists to spiritual healers, but I pass. I will have to work out the solutions myself.

Perhaps, I imagine, my body is sending me a message by refusing to settle. It is time to sort myself out, not just physically but mentally. My injuries will heal, I hope, but I also need to put my mind at rest.

The prospects for discovering my birth details are better than ever. For the first time, my adoption agency has given me information from my file; very limited information, it is true, but there are leads in there that I can follow up. Separately, just as I am stepping up my inquiries, society is finally ready to lower the veil of secrecy that has existed around adoption for so long.

I hope, too, that Olive might still fill in some of the blanks in my history. To no avail. The opportunity to raise the matter with her never arises, or my efforts are too ineffectual to produce a result. I try to ask questions during my infrequent phone calls to her, but she always closes down discussion of the issue.

She does send me a poignant letter, in which she finds it marginally easier to express herself. 'I would love to have kept you but found [it] nearly impossible as I had to go to work,' she wrote me. 'Eventually they found a place in a Foster Home in Dublin with a lovely lady. It nearly broke my heart to part with you.'

It is a rare moment when she feels free enough to speak from the heart.

35

On the day I enter the world, I am placed on my back on a tray, my tiny arms and legs akimbo. Wrapped in muslin cloth, I have the head of a mini-Winston Churchill: purple, furrowed brow; eyes scrunched up under the bright light, mere lines behind rolls of flesh; fists raised in mute protest. My mouth forms a perfect O, a hangover from the shock I feel from the metal of the tray running cold against my smooth skin.

The tray starts to rise as a nurse, dressed in starched white dress and white cap, heaps balancing weights on the other side of the scales. She places ten individual pound weights on a second tray, the last causing my side to lurch violently upwards. She removes one of the cast-iron discs, and I plummet. Now she slips on eleven single-ounce weights, one by one. More gently now, my tray rises. Through the mysteries of gravity, the scales reach a steady equilibrium. The nurse scratches a note in her file as I slip peacefully into sleep.

Looking up from the page, it takes me a second to realise I am not in a hospital, not back in the 1960s. My mind has raced ahead of the words I am reading, building on their raw detail to create a mental picture of my first day on Earth.

'You were born on May 11th 1963 at Whittington Hospital. Your birth weight was 9lbs 11ozs' – the first words of the file that has been thrust in my hands.

Prosaic details. But this middle-aged adult has until now known nothing about the circumstances of his birth, aside from the date. No descriptions, no photographs. But now at least I have a written account. Eyelids quivering, I struggle to focus on the words. It is easier to indulge myself in the fantasy of a helpless, tiny me being measured on an old-fashioned weighing scales.

'You had blue eyes, dark hair, fair skin and were described as "a big baby" with "rather coarse features",' I read. 'You were born on a Saturday, and spent eleven days in the maternity wing of the hospital.'

Saturday's child works hard for a living, goes the rhyme. I search for a time of birth – never too late to develop an interest in astrology – but none is given.

The document is based on what Olive told nurses at the time of my birth. About my father, it says: 'She named him as Vincent Duffy and said he was twenty-six years of age, Irish from Monaghan and of the Roman Catholic faith. He was a policeman living and working in Dublin. Olive described him as being six feet tall, with fair hair, blue eyes and fair skin.'

It had taken a lot of time and some digging to gain access to this information. Not in Dublin, but in London. At home, my adoption agency, Cúnamh, would tell me no more. Not until it was forced to by a change in the law, and that appeared unlikely.

The 'who, what, where and when' of my past was becoming clearer but the 'why' remained as elusive as ever. However, re-examining the sparse material provided by the agency turned up a potential lead. When Olive was pregnant with me in London, it mentioned, she was in contact with an organisation known as the Crusade of Rescue. Despite the strange name, it was a British adoption agency, with links to the CPRSI/Cúnamh back in Dublin. Furthermore, it was still in existence, known now as the Catholic Children's Society.

Founded in 1859 with the full name of the Crusade of Rescue and Homes for Destitute Catholic Children, the society ran orphanages and children's homes in England until the 1970s. Between 1948 and 2008, it placed over 6,000 children with adoptive families, according to its website.

I fired off a hopeful email to the society and received a prompt response. A helpful administrator promised to search her archives.

She did unearth a file on Olive and me, covering the time we fell under its care. But there was a fly in the ointment. Under the charity's quirky rules, information could be imparted only at a face-to-face interview. I would have to travel to England. And the waiting time was seven months.

Still, this English agency might prove to be more transparent than its equivalent in Dublin. In contrast to the foot-dragging in Ireland, adopted children in the UK won the legal right to obtain their birth and adoption records in 1975, with the Crusade of Rescue lobbying in favour of the change at that time.

The accident in Germany forced me to postpone a visit to the agency, but by the following spring I had recovered sufficiently from my injuries to be able to fly again. When an invitation arrived for the wedding of friends in London, I made an appointment to visit the Catholic Children's Society the day before the big event.

I had few expectations, having been in enough meetings with guarded social workers by then not to get my hopes up. I was mindful, too, that the time I had spent in England was short – about four months – compared to the years I had spent in care in Ireland.

The agency is located in modern, bright offices in a settled residential area of north London, a pleasing contrast to the gloomy atmosphere at the CPRSI. Here I was, sitting across the table with yet another social worker, but this one started by apologising profusely for the delay in seeing me. She then handed me a thick folder summarising my involvement with the agency. More detailed than the information I was given in Dublin, it started with the moment of my birth.

As with my adoption agency in Dublin, the Catholic Children's Society was not prepared to release my file, but the folder contained copies of original documents rather than mere summaries of their contents. I got a richer sense of the unfolding events as I was shuttled from place to place.

Crucially, this chronology of my earliest movements contained the information I was looking for, allowing me to fill in another piece of the jigsaw. In London, Olive and I were sent to a mother and baby home after our time in hospital, it confirmed. I knew that already.

But here for the first time, I learned the name of the home and its location – St Pelagia's in north London, my first address.

36

I grew up without the habit of seeking versions of myself in the faces and characters of those around me. It often felt like me against the world. This made me both stronger and more fragile. I was ruggedly individualistic, and yet I lacked resilience. I was a risk-taker, and a worrier. I lacked a roadmap for the future that others could divine by just looking at their parents. Sometimes, I imagine, this can be an advantage.

A sense of difference is a two-way phenomenon. My adoptive parents must undoubtedly have been conscious of how different I looked from them. My mother, a woman well acquainted with arguing that black was white, would insist on our close resemblance to anyone she happened to meet. 'Isn't he the spit of me?' she would announce to the polite bemusement of strangers, and my growing mortification over the years. The last time I heard her use this expression, she reached no higher than my midriff.

Having met my birth mother, though, I could no longer pretend that I wasn't related to anyone. My relationship with Olive remained halting and distant, but over time I developed a warm friendship with her two daughters, who were more than a decade younger than me.

At first, it was strange to be meeting people who shared my genetic lineage. Adopted people, assuming they are aware they are adopted, are generally not in the habit of looking for similarities in the people around them. They know they don't look like their parents, will not age like them and may not die of the same diseases. We are all fundamentally alone in the world, but adopted people learn this earlier and know it better than most.

Meeting Olive and my half-sisters, I was finally confronted with my likeness, at least in part. I was taller than anyone on this side of the family, but particular attributes – the grey hair, the oval face – marked me down as a member of her family.

When I first met her, I had been anxious not to pry. Out of loyalty to my adoptive parents, I felt I might be letting them down by inquiring about my birth mother's life story, thereby entertaining a 'what-might-have-been' scenario. Later, I did pose a few gentle questions, but gave up quickly because of the lack of information she was willing to provide. Olive is used to people talking over her in company. I struggled on my occasional visits to find a private moment when she might open up.

This suited her, I suspected. She didn't want to revisit what had happened before I was born, not even for my sake.

Now I resolved to put my questions to her directly. To ensure there were no distractions or interruptions, I invited her out to lunch at a gastro-pub near where she lived.

Olive was by this time in her early eighties. She was as quiet as ever, and still reluctant to have someone poke around in her past. At this stage she could be forgiven for not remembering everything that happened half a century before. Or was she so conditioned to not sharing her secret that she couldn't change now? It was hard to tell.

Pressed for the first time by direct questions from me, she recited what I already knew. My father was a garda, she hadn't seen him since the 1960s and she went to London to give birth to me. She declined to elaborate, not even by providing emotional colour or any of those small, telling details of biography that might give me an understanding of what happened. Instead, she leaned on platitudes about the 'hard times' her generation had lived through. Well, they seemed like platitudes to me, even if true.

The world had changed a lot since I first heard adoption being discussed on radio chat shows in the 1970s. The personal tragedies of those affected, especially vulnerable young birth mothers who gave up their children, were widely covered in the media. There was also coverage of adopted adults seeking to make contact with their genetic parents and, to a much lesser extent, adoptive parents struggling with the challenges of raising a child.

Over those forty-plus years, sentimentality had, understandably, given way to anger. The secrecy that underpinned adoption came under attack. Respect for the Catholic Church collapsed under the weight of successive scandals; its historical role in managing extra-marital births drew increasingly critical scrutiny. No-one was angrier, albeit with more cause than most, than the community of adopted people – the 'bastard nation', as US activists styled themselves. In the past, the emphasis had been on secrecy. Now it was on personal rights, particularly the right to one's identity. For adoptees, this started with the names of their parents.

Channelling some of this anger, I decided to press Olive more forcefully about my father. Previously, I had merely scratched at the surface, with polite requests. Now I tried to insist on my right to be told more.

My efforts were in vain. So much time had passed. She talked vaguely of meet-ups and dances with my father but could provide no specifics. She could not, or would not, remember anything of the look of him, the amount of time they were together or whether he had brothers or sisters that she also knew. Vincent Duffy remained a riddle. I wondered if he even existed.

By the time her steak arrived, she asked that we change the subject. We talked about the weather and the food.

I was enormously disheartened after this meeting. Yet it reminded me how little I knew about Olive. After more than twenty years of meeting on and off, she remained a mystery to me.

I was by now familiar with the basic facts of her life. Her

birth mother was a middle child of ten from a family in rural Ireland. She described her father as a hard man, a disciplinarian, who had spent time in the United States before returning to farm in Ireland, just before the Great Crash.

The defining event of her early life was her mother's death, when she was still a child. Her parents were shopping in the local town one day when her mother, who was in her forties, suffered a severe heart attack and died. 'My dad got a big shock and I suppose he lost interest in us to some extent,' she explained matter-of-factly.

Leaving school early, Olive was sent to Dublin to work in a grocery shop. Through her teens, she continued to work in various shops in the capital, though it was not to her liking: 'I was the quietest in the house [and] hated shop work.'

At eighteen, she began working in a psychiatric hospital. 'That really got me down. I became like one of the patients. Even after I left there ten months later, my life was wrecked for years,' she admitted in one of her letters.

At this time, Ireland incarcerated more of its population in asylums than any other country. Conditions in these ageing institutions were dreadful. It was hardly the best career choice for someone with her fragile background but, as she reminded me, options were limited in 1950s Ireland, especially for women.

She travelled to England with her younger sister, Patricia, and the pair trained in general nursing in Liverpool.

Patricia has happy memories of the time they spent together in England. 'She was in great demand, our Olive, always a line of suitors coming to her door,' she told me. 'She was great craic too. She had a laugh as big as the Albert Hall.'

Olive experienced this as a darker time. '[I] worked there for four years, though I developed mental illness so [it] was a battle to pass exams,' she told me in another letter, which arrived unsolicited after one of my intermittent attempts to prise some detail from her about my story. Though she was steadfast in remaining silent, it was clear she suffered guilt.

She returned home after a few years working as a nurse in England because she was homesick, but had to head there again after becoming pregnant with me.

Patricia couldn't shed any light on the circumstances of my conception. 'I didn't know – about you – at the time,' she said. 'Then Olive and I had a disagreement one day, which was very unusual, and out she came with it – that she had given birth to a child. But she wouldn't say much. I do remember her needing to borrow money, which was also very unusual.' I explained that this was probably needed for my upkeep.

Olive endured a difficult few years after I was placed in foster care and then adoption. In 1966, the year I was formally adopted, she suffered a breakdown while working as a nurse in London. Returning to Dublin, she spent six months in hospital. She was on 'a lot of tablets'.

'It wasn't the easiest part of my life,' she told me once, with characteristic understatement.

She resumed working as a nurse in a small hospital outside Dublin but found it tiring as her treatment continued. Despite her troubles, she met someone, a man from her own part of the country: 'We were to get engaged but I would be moving in with his sister also when we wed. He knew I was worried [about that] as I was still on treatment and he broke it off.'

This disappointment made her fatalistic about ever meeting a partner. Then she saw a newspaper advertisement for a marriage bureau and contacted it. Through this twentieth-century version of a dating app, she met her future husband in 1970. The couple wed in her home county shortly after. They settled down and had four children, including two boys who have lived in the US for many years.

I came to know well the view out of Olive's window on my visits to her home. There, in the heart of Ireland, I would tuck into her ham and cheese sandwiches, gazing out on low hills while a clock's ticking filled the room. She must have spent many dusky evenings watching the rain pelt down on these fields, I thought, all the time wondering where I was.

One late summer's day, I brought my young children on a visit. Watching their joyful play on the golden rolls of hay that dotted the fields out the back set me thinking about that separated past. There were times in her life, I knew, when these fields were filled with the shouts and smiles of her other children, as it was with mine on this evening. But, for Olive, the joy of those days must have been suffused with sadness, knowing her first-born child was far away.

37

St Pelagia's Home for Penitent Girls, my address for the first month of my life, has been described as the world's first mother and baby home. It began caring for single mothers in 1889, according to an information leaflet provided by the Catholic Children's Society. Over eight decades, it sent thousands of their children for adoption. Many of these were Irish.

As for St Pelagia, she is the subject of multiple, largely apocryphal stories from the mists of time. The patron saint of actresses, she is said to have been a fifteen-year-old Christian virgin from the fourth century who threw herself from a housetop to save her chastity, dying instantly. According to another myth, she is St Pelagia the Harlot, a prostitute who converted suddenly to Christianity and went to live an ascetic life in a cave in Jerusalem, disguised as a man.

By the colourful account of one website, St Pelagia was the living embodiment of the goddess Aphrodite and, until she reformed herself, 'the most notorious prostitute in Antioch, so beautiful in fact that no carnal man could take his eyes off her'.

Another fictitious St Pelagia was supposedly roasted to death for refusing to marry the Roman emperor Diocletian.

Whether Pelagia was a prostitute turned ascetic, or a teen virgin killing herself to preserve her chastity, the message to the women coming into the home was clear enough: you who have fallen must save yourselves.

St Pelagia's was run by the Sisters of the Sacred Hearts of Jesus and Mary, the same congregation that ran Sean Ross Abbey in County Tipperary and the notorious Bessborough home in Cork. Infant mortality rates at Bessborough were shockingly high; they averaged 25 per cent between the mid-1930s and mid-1950s, peaking at 75 per cent in 1943. At least 923 children died over the seventy-six years the home was in operation.

In 1924, St Pelagia's moved to a 10-acre site at a Sacred Hearts convent on a hill in Highgate, north London. This was where I came with Olive after being discharged from hospital.

The nuns' links across the Irish Sea were long established. As St Pelagia's was being set up in Highgate, a representative of the home visited Ireland to discuss opening a mother and baby home in Dublin for unmarried mothers. The home planned to segregate 'first offender mothers, who are generally of a decent class, from the vast number who were, generally, old offenders', a poor law commissioner told the *Irish Independent*.

Black-and-white pictures of the home in Highgate show an imposing house built on classical lines, a neatly trimmed lawn out front and a statue of Christ in beseeching mode facing the entrance to the home. There is another old photo, clearly posed, of a neat playroom, where infants in white clothes sit on rocking horses and on the floor, watched over by stern carers in starched white gowns with elaborate headgear. There was once a garden, which provided food for the residents, but it had disappeared by the time Olive got there.

At any one time, St Pelagia's nursery was home to fifty to sixty babies, most of them the children of Irish women. The nursery was divided into sections with eight to ten babies each. Mothers would come to feed babies at regular intervals before leaving them again to the care of the nuns and other staff.

Most of the referrals to St Pelagia's came from the Crusade of Rescue, with the local authority picking up the tab for the mothers' care. To generate extra income, the home took in washing from large houses in the area, which the mothers were forced to wash in return for their keep. The laundry closed in 1954, in contrast to the laundries in Irish mother and baby homes which survived for another few decades.

Mothers generally stayed six weeks before giving birth, and six weeks after it. There was an obstetrician on call, according to the Crusade of Rescue, but 'on occasion', where medically indicated, mothers were transferred to Whittington Hospital on Holloway Road to give birth.

Was I such an occasion, I wondered. My file didn't say whether Olive was routinely transferred to the state-run hospital for my birth or whether this was because of a medical emergency. But I did have a forceps delivery.

'The women were often given different first names in order to preserve their confidentiality,' the information sheet provided by the adoption agency told me. Former residents have confirmed this in discussions in online chat forums, with one describing the atmosphere in the home as 'very hush-hush'.

In common with other homes, mortality rates in St Pelagia's were much higher than in the wider community. The apparatus used to contain unmarried mothers and their children in homes has received far less scrutiny in the UK than in Ireland. In December 2024 ITN News reported that thirty-seven babies who died in St Pelagia's were buried in unmarked plots nearby.

I subsequently obtained the list of these babies, twenty-seven of whom had recognisably Irish names. Four were marked as stillborns. The lifespan of the other babies was measured in minutes, hours, weeks or months – from two minutes up to six months.

The home gets mixed reviews from those who spent time there. The daughter of one resident claimed it was 'like a boarding school' and said the mothers were treated very well. Most other contributors to an online discussion forum disagreed, with one describing it as 'hell on earth' when she stayed there in 1967.

'We were sinners and the nuns made sure we knew that. There were so many sad stories,' said another woman who stayed in St Pelagia's when giving birth that year.

'It was no holiday home. We weren't mistreated but we were

reminded every morning we got up what an awful thing we had done by the nuns. It was no walk in the park. I hated it and we had to work hard in the kitchen and around,' another former resident recalled.

When this criticism was aired publicly in the British media, the Catholic Children's Society pleaded for the practices at St Pelagia's not to be judged by contemporary standards. 'What we now know happened in Ireland, if true, was appalling,' the society's chief executive Rosemary Keenan said in 2016. 'But I don't think that's what was happening at St Pelagia's. Where possible, mothers were supported by us in keeping their children. But there was pressure at the time on young single women who became pregnant. Many would have had difficulties with societal and their own families' disapproving attitude to single mothers.'

If mothers were supported to keep their children, as claimed, they have yet to come forward. And if Olive was offered support to keep me, it is not recorded in my files. Nothing she has said since points to this having happened.

I was bottle-fed, according to my file. Curious to know if other children were breast-fed, I put the question on an online chat group for former residents. All who replied said they had been bottle-fed. The nuns were anxious to discourage bonding between mothers and their babies, one mother told me. Another said she was told bottle-feeding was easier to manage: 'The babies were fed by their mothers at set times, according to age. At these times, mothers would report to the nursery and feed, change and play with the babies. Between these times, two of the mothers would be on "nursery duty" and would look after any baby that was crying. There wouldn't have been enough nuns to feed all the babies.'

St Pelagia's remained open as late as 1971. This was four years after abortion was legalised in the UK. After it closed, the site was sold and redeveloped into residential accommodation. I walked around the area on my trip to London to pick up information at the Catholic Children's Society. The part of north London where I spent my first weeks of life is now an affluent suburb, not far from Hampstead Heath. The former mother and baby home site today houses a gated block of flats hidden behind a discreet high wall. Apartments in the complex sell for millions of pounds.

Highgate Cemetery nearby has been extended to cover some of the site of the former mother and baby home. Many years before, on my birthday, I visited the grave of Karl Marx in the cemetery, never realising that I had spent time as a tiny newborn in a mother and baby home just a stone's throw away, at the same time of the year.

St Pelagia's was run with military precision. As with the Irish mother and baby homes, there was a huge emphasis on raising revenue. London County Council footed much of the cost, but was desperate to relieve itself of the burden of hosting this influx of pregnant young women from Ireland. Mothers were discharged quickly, most often back to Ireland. Around the time I was there, the council was paying a guinea (21 shillings) a week to the home for expectant mothers and 25 shillings for mothers and babies. Many of the babies were sent to mother and baby homes in Ireland run by the Sisters of the Sacred Hearts of Jesus and Mary.

Theoretically, the women passing through St Pelagia's were free to decide on the fate of their babies, but in practice they were under tremendous pressure to have them adopted. The Catholic Church was bent on the avoidance of scandal and ensuring that babies born to Irish unmarried mothers were adopted by Catholic families. Local authorities in Britain were determined that the women and their children did not become burdens on the taxpayer. And where the women told their families about their pregnancy, they were invariably presented with adoption as the solution.

As a result, the adoptions that took place from homes such as St Pelagia's are today routinely described as forced. The Scottish and Welsh administrations have apologised for forced adoptions but the UK government has yet to do so.

I spent a month at St Pelagia's, the records show, as Olive presumably was working out what to do with me. My birth was formally registered while I was there.

Armed with the information I had obtained in London, I applied to the General Register Office in the UK for a copy of my birth certificate. For most people, this is a straightforward document, but in Ireland the birth certificates of adopted people remained secret. Not so in Britain; mine arrived in the post within days, more than half a century after my birth was registered. It lists Olive, a state registered nurse, as my mother. The address where she was staying before and after my birth is listed coyly under 'residence of informant' as 34 Highgate West Hill, London. This is St Pelagia's, though the home is not mentioned by name. Disappointingly for me, the column for 'father' has a line drawn through it.

So, while I was not born in an actual mother and baby home, it is fair to say that I was born *into* one. I was baptised in the home three days after admission, by a priest in the chapel of the Sacred Hearts convent.

Olive had arrived in England at the start of her pregnancy, according to the file I was given. She had previously trained as a nurse in Liverpool and went to work in Dublin. 'Pregnancy took place there', according to the records, and she travelled back to England in October 1962. Her father was unaware of the pregnancy. (Her mother was long dead at this point.)

My birth was marked down as 'illegitimate' – the other choices were 'legitimate', 'legitimated' and 'extramarital'.

Though I read this questionnaire many times after receiving it, for a long while I failed to spot the most remarkable nugget of information it contained.

There, tucked away in a box on the right-hand side of the first page, was an indication that I was part of something bigger, a malign form of 'underground railroad' that had been created long before Olive or I ever came to St Pelagia's.

In answer to a question on 'other societies or agencies involved' was written simply: 'P.F.I.' Pregnant from Ireland. Here, in this tiny note, added to her record almost as an afterthought, was proof that Olive's experience of being tossed over and back between two countries was one shared by many other unmarried mothers from Ireland. They even had a shorthand for them. For the first time, I felt I was dealing with a wider, more structured and more deliberate apparatus of containment of unmarried mothers, not just in Ireland but also in Britain.

38

'A six-month-old baby was in a cramped Moses-type basket,' the journalist wrote. 'Another in a carrycot inside an ordinary cot had his own sick all over his clothes. It had caked dry on him.'

'I like to have a good selection here,' the widow who ran the foster home was quoted as saying, 'so that when people come they have a few to choose from for adoption. It saves them going away disappointed and getting a baby somewhere else.'

The line might have come from Charles Dickens. But the year was 1968, and a British Sunday newspaper was on the trail of a 'baby farm' in north Dublin. Accompanying the journalist was a mother who found that the baby she had repatriated and put up for adoption was now living with eight others in terrible conditions in this house.

'The stench was awful,' the newspaper reported. 'Cobwebs hung from the ceiling' and cots in what the widow called 'the nursery' were covered in dirt. In one battered pink cot was an eighteen-month-old 'coloured' boy lying on a torn and pitted foam mattress. There were no sheets on the mattress, the only covering was a tiny piece of blanket in one corner and the home had not been inspected before the babies were placed there.

Westminster City Council, which had paid for the woman and her baby to be sent back to Ireland, said the allegations had been thoroughly investigated, and proved to be unfounded. But the newspaper doubled down on its claims the following week, accusing the council of doing a 'quick clean-up job' after the allegations emerged. There was no piped water or drainage system in the village where the home was located, it pointed out, and the owner of the foster home drew her water from a pump 75 yards away.

It was hard to see how anyone could maintain hygiene in these conditions, but the foster mother, who had five children of her own in the house, insisted that she had been able to keep all her charges warm and fed. 'It's just as though they were in hospital,' she said. 'They just lie in their own cots quietly and are no trouble at all.'

'The conditions are not 100 per cent, but you can't judge these things by English standards,' a London County Council official told the journalist, with no sense of embarrassment.

A chill went through me, reading this allegation of severe neglect in a foster home, dating from the period when I was in one. The mother at the centre of the story had believed her baby was being well cared for pending a speedy adoption, but found him living in dirty, unsanitary conditions. Was this my experience of fostering? Could I ever be assured that I had not suffered similar neglect? I needed to find out as much as I could about my own foster care.

My research into PFIs left me gobsmacked. Why on earth was an English local authority funding foster care in a north Dublin cottage, as was the case according to the newspaper article I had come across?

By now, everyone was familiar with the harsh treatment unmarried mothers endured in the church-dominated Ireland of the mid-twentieth century. But these women were also mistreated in supposedly liberal England, and, by virtue of being shuttled between countries, they were shunned in both.

The article caused a brief flurry of hand-wringing, before the blanket of denial descended once again. PFIs were almost never mentioned. It wasn't until the report of the Irish government's mother and baby home commission was published in 2021 that their plight received attention.

Reading about the PFIs, I came to see the term as shorthand for a two-way system of people smuggling. It meant babies born to unmarried Irish Catholic women remained hidden, remained Catholic and, largely, went back to Ireland. Thousands of these women were whisked over to Britain, to give birth out of sight. Their babies were then given up for adoption to Catholic families back in Ireland. While the system was driven by

Catholic adoption agencies, it couldn't have happened without the connivance of both states.

It was hard not to be angry at the scale of the phenomenon. Some 2,434 PFIs and their babies were funded to return to Ireland between 1948 and 1971, but gaps in official data meant that the real figure is likely to be far higher. As many as 10,000 women and babies may have been deported from Britain to Ireland in this way, ITN News estimated in 2025. This was based on official records and the claim by Father James Good, the priest who was heavily involved in arranging the adoption of children born to Irish unmarried mothers in Britain, that 8–10,000 Irish women travelled to England to have their babies because they were not married. Father Good, no doubt convinced of his own nominative determinism, boasted that he 'handled' the transport of 954 babies from England for adoption in Cork over a twelve-year period in the 1950s and 1960s.

England was an obvious destination for young single pregnant Irish women, the mother and baby homes report pointed out. In an era of high emigration, an announcement by a woman that she was travelling across the Irish Sea was unlikely to attract questions (so long as the pregnancy was concealed).

'We have no concept of the shame in those days of having a baby outside marriage,' the late Father Good told the *Sunday Independent* in 2014. 'The family would often throw them out or her mother would take her to England and say "you stay there now until you get rid of it". A parish priest would tell her "get out, you're a disgrace". A man in those days ... if he didn't put his name on the birth cert, he didn't exist.'

'The dreadful fear of these mothers, scared they'd be seen ... In the early days, there was very little bonding between the mother and child. They wanted to get rid of the baby, as simple as that. There wasn't a great deal of emotion,' Father Good recounted in an earlier interview, in 2005.

He recalled conversations with the administrator of the Crusade of Rescue: 'Westminster Diocese had 500 Irish girls a year, steady, dropping their babies on their doorstep. And he'd ring me up late at night. "[Father] Good, two bloody PFIs arrived on my doorstep this morning. Can you handle them?" And another night, he rings me up: "[Father] Good, hope you're well. We have two babies here. I want to get them adopted fast. Can you take them tomorrow morning?"'

The administrator rushing these babies across the Irish Sea in such cavalier a fashion was Canon Philip Harvey, I noted. I too had been 'dropped on his doorstep' and then trafficked by his adoption agency to Ireland.

Initially, the young Irish girls fleeing to England were well received. 'What have we to offer her here [in Ireland] in comparison with the concealment, comfort and facility for adoption offered in Great Britain?' Alice Litster, a government-appointed inspector of mother and baby homes, asked in a

1948 report. 'In this country [Britain] she can obtain shelter during her waiting time, good food and care, skilled attention during confinement, care, attention and kindness to her baby.'

But the welcome evaporated over time. British charities pressurised the Irish Catholic hierarchy and the Irish state to repatriate pregnant Irish women. Movement across the Irish Sea was more 'push' from England than 'pull' from Dublin, according to academic Paul Michael Garrett.

'One aspect of the PFI story that has gone largely unnoticed,' the mother and baby homes report pointed out, 'was the return to Ireland by British social services and British Catholic charities of children who were born in Britain to Irish mothers. It is highly unlikely that unmarried mothers did not experience some hostility/prejudice on occasion.'

Back at home, the fleeing PFIs were a source of 'national embarrassment', according to historian Lindsey Earner-Byrne, and the repatriation scheme was motivated by shame.

The system suited societies on both sides of the Irish Sea, but there were arguments about funding. In 1931, Ireland agreed to cover half the cost of sending women home with their babies, the first time the state agreed to take responsibility for a group of its emigrants.

These money rows went on for years. In 1939, Catholic Archbishop of Westminster Cardinal Arthur Hinsley complained to Taoiseach Éamon de Valera about almost 100 pregnant Irish women 'intending to leave (their) child in England as a charge upon the generosity of English Catholics'. He suggested the women became pregnant because 'sheer weakness of intellect and character combined with inexperience is often the cause of their downfall'.

Cardinal Hinsley called on the Irish government to match the grant London County Council paid for each Irish 'inmate' in Catholic mother and baby homes. He also demanded the CPRSI do more to take children born to the women back to Ireland.

With the Irish government reluctant to support the women, this job fell to a largely reluctant Catholic hierarchy. It in turn pushed responsibility onto voluntary organisations. They focused on first-time unmarried mothers who had conceived children in Ireland; women deemed to be 'multiple offenders' were not included. Initially, the government stumped up 50 per cent of the costs involved, but before long the church had taken over completely; its voluntary agencies were not slow about getting the women, Olive included, to pay the costs involved.

The CPRSI, the agency that arranged my adoption, was assigned responsibility for repatriating Catholic Irish unmarried mothers in 1941, as Garrett noted, 'at the special request of the Cardinal and Archbishops of Ireland'. War might have been raging in Europe but the church was moving with alacrity to set up a system to save the souls of the PFI babies. Staff would meet the repatriated woman, with her child, on their arrival in Dublin or another Irish port and transport them to a mother and baby home. I wondered if this had happened to me.

The number of PFIs increased after the Second World War, peaking at 213 in 1967. In 1963, Olive, with me in her arms, was one of 135 PFIs repatriated via my adoption agency to Ireland.

Shockingly, the women who arrived from Ireland during pregnancy were denied access to the British National Health Service. Theoretically, they were entitled to treatment, but the local authorities providing maternity care did not necessarily follow NHS guidelines. Ireland was not the only immigrant community 'targeted' in this manner; the Colonial Office actively escorted the children of unmarried West Indian immigrants back to the Caribbean.

As the stream of PFIs continued unabated, British authorities redoubled their efforts to shunt Irish girls back home. From the 1950s, London County Council placed an official for six months a year in Ireland looking for homes for the repatriated children, based in the CPRSI offices in Dublin. The council hoped parents would be less likely to encourage their daughters to travel to England if they thought the children would be sent back to Ireland. But as the Sunday newspaper revelations showed, some of these children ended up in unregulated foster care.

Looking at the agencies that assumed responsibility for my care in those early years, I could see that a clue as to their real purpose was in the name: the Crusade of Rescue in England, and the Catholic Protection and Rescue Society of Ireland (CPRSI) in Dublin.

Rescue? *From what* was clear enough; *for what*, less so. 'The dominant ethos within the Church was to place the avoidance of scandal above the welfare of children,' according to journalist and author Mike Milotte.

'The mission of the CPRSI and St Patrick's Guild, and British societies such as the Crusade of Rescue, was to prevent Catholic infants becoming Protestants and to rescue women who were believed to be in danger of losing their Catholic faith,' the mother and baby homes report noted. 'The CPRSI assisted any case where there appeared to be a risk that a child would not be raised as a Catholic.' That, in effect, meant that any case involving the birth in Britain of a child to an unmarried Irish woman.

Olive was far from being the first Irish woman to end up in London hiding an extra-marital birth. For decades, this well-oiled network had been in existence to ensure that these babies could be born out of sight overseas and then funnelled back to Ireland for adoption in good Irish families.

Asked in 2025 about the treatment meted out to PFIs, the Catholic Children's Society told ITN News: 'Many young mothers in the past felt they had no choice but to place their child for adoption due to the stigma of being unmarried and the lack of support available to them from the government, their families and wider society at the time. This is deeply regrettable and a tragedy for all involved.'

The mother and baby home report devoted a chapter to the personal histories of unmarried women who became pregnant in Ireland in the mid-twentieth century. 'Women who became pregnant outside marriage faced a series of crises: homelessness, loss of employment, destitution, possible rejection by their family,' it concluded. 'Mother and baby homes provided immediate relief from these challenges, but these women had *little if any choice* [my emphasis] about the long-term future of their child. Few women at this time earned enough money to support themselves and their child, and even fewer would have had the confidence to withstand the opprobrium that they would face, from family, neighbours and society.'

This was the range of forces bearing down on Olive as she tried to decide what to do with me. She needed privacy and secrecy. The Catholic Church wanted to ensure that I didn't end up with a Protestant family. So did its adoption agencies in Dublin and London. They demanded money from her to fund their work. London County Council did not care where I ended up, so long as it was back in Ireland, off their books. None of these agencies was looking after my best interests. Olive was surely one of those women identified in the report who had 'little if any choice'. I understood now: she could never have hoped to keep me.

39

I once mentioned the fact of my adoption in a phone call with a colleague in *The Irish Times*, the late Kathryn Holmquist. A sympathetic and inquisitive writer, Kathryn materialised by my desk within minutes, asking to interview me for a feature.

The suggestion sent me into the horrors. Even the thought of going public was anathema to me at this time, when my mother was alive. I had met Olive by then, so I felt I was walking a very fine tightrope between potentially competing relationships. And so I sent my colleague packing, knowing she was never short of good interviewees.

And while I did ultimately embark on a search for answers, it remained a private undertaking for many years. If I wanted to fill in the blanks in my own story, that was for my benefit, my eyes, only.

That changed after I learned about Olive and all the other PFIs. Here was an obvious wrong, I felt, a story that needed to be told. The thousands of women who were shuttled between Ireland and Britain and Ireland again simply because they were unmarried and pregnant had been forgotten, despite all the attention given to mother and baby homes and other Catholic-run institutions.

I was still no adoption advocate, but I started taking a greater interest in the work of those who were. All the time I was investigating my past, the debate raged on around adoption, focusing as ever on the balance between the rights of adopted people and the mothers who bore them.

The door had long stayed shut on providing adoptees with information about their birth. To do so, it was argued, could infringe the right to privacy of their birth mothers. Any attempt to override the right to privacy would fall foul of Ireland's constitution, we were repeatedly told. And since there was no prospect of it being amended to provide birth information, adoptees remained lumped with the status quo.

Or so it seemed. As Catholic Church scandals continued to multiply and public opinion shifted, politicians became more receptive to change. What was said to be impossible gradually became a possibility.

In 1998, the Supreme Court rejected a claim by an adult adoptee that the secrecy around adoption in Ireland was unconstitutional. A birth mother's right to privacy superseded an adoptee's right to information, the court ruled in a landmark judgement. The records kept by adoption agencies remained sealed. They were to stay that way for decades more.

Adoptees had to make the running themselves, with shoestring resources. When the first Irish online register to facilitate contact between people affected by adoption was launched in 1999, it was sponsored by a supermarket chain.

Successive proposals were made to give legal recognition to an adopted person's right to their identity, but none succeeded. In 2001, for example, a new bill proposed opening up access to records but threatened adoptees who tried to contact their birth parents without permission with a year in jail. It was dropped after an outcry.

Thanks to the internet, it was a good time to be searching for a lost family. Adopted friends started telling me how they had used digitised information – from birth and death records to newspaper archives – to trace their origins. They took to online chat groups to share experiences and develop techniques for parsing the huge amounts of data newly available.

Legislatively, nothing substantive happened for more than a decade, yet there was an urgency about resolving the issue. Adoption numbers had peaked in 1967, when almost 1,500 children were formally adopted – 97 per cent of all 'illegitimate' children born that year. This meant that the major generation of birth mothers who had given up their children was now well into old age.

Then came *Philomena*, released in 2013, the moving account of Philomena Lee's fifty-year search for her lost son. Wiping my tears away as the credits rolled, I remembered that the nuns at Sean Ross Abbey, who had thwarted Philomena's search at every turn, were the same secretive congregation that ran St Pelagia's in London.

In the film's aftermath, the pace of change picked up. Successive proposals were brought forward by legislators, but rejected by advocates as inadequate.

I was becoming more mindful of my own right to information but I was also conscious that Olive had embraced secrecy with regard to my father's identity. In 2019, Katharine Zappone, one of a succession of ministers for children given responsibility for the issue, released correspondence she had received from individual birth mothers. One woman, who signed her letter as a 'terrified mother', told the minister she had given up her child for adoption fifty years earlier. Her siblings knew nothing about her 'sin'.

'What do I do now?' the woman asked. 'I have no rights. And for the second time, I have no say in what is to happen when the files are thrown open and I'm outed as a heartless woman. So please will you say something to us? What are we supposed to do?'

It was a rare moment when the often forgotten voices of an earlier generation – cowed birth mothers cleaving to their right to secrecy – were heard. In them, I heard echoes of my adoptive mother's insecurities and my birth mother's pieties.

'We cannot have a law that provides unrestricted access to information about one's identity to the adopted person,' Zappone concluded. 'I will not be bringing in amendments that provide for unrestricted access. I cannot do that as a minister with the legal officer of the government, the attorney general, saying that you can't do that.'

Yet within a few years, a later government would do exactly that – or very close to it.

40

I was no closer to understanding the mystery of my early years. My birth mother had closed the book on it and my files remained with my adoption agency in Dublin, unavailable to me. Perhaps if I was able to track down my genetic father, it might help to unlock it.

And so I found myself, on a cold day in 2019, in the research room of the General Register Office (GRO) on Werburgh Street in Dublin, trying to piece together his identity from the scant information I had in my possession. Maybe my search would succeed where the one done by my adoption agency had not.

As the name indicates, the GRO holds registers – huge, bound ledgers – of historical Irish births, deaths and marriages. Each volume contains an index list of the records for a particular year or area. Users present a chit at the information desk requesting a particular volume. After a short wait, staff carry the requested volume to their table.

Entering the large, dimly lit room, I was struck by its air of hushed solemnity. Researchers had been beating a path to the GRO for many years, seeking to pierce the wall of secrecy around adoption. By tracking birth and death records and combining them with known snippets of information, some had successfully traced family members. A birth mother searching for a long-lost child, for example, would go through the laborious exercise of searching the records for all children born on the same day as her child. This list, shortened by excluding boys' or girls' names as appropriate, could then be cross-checked with the records of adoption orders listed in the government publication *Iris Oifigiúil*. The adopted child, obviously, bore a new surname and might also have a new first name. However, it could yet be possible to make a closer match if any other information was provided by the adoption agency.

I had read *Unspoken*, a novel by Anne Harris, who gave up her first child for adoption when she was a student. In the book, the central birth mother character was able to pick out her adopted son from a list of people born on his birth date because she had been told he bore an Irish first name.

The GRO used to be an unwelcoming place for people carrying out such searches. In the past, users were not allowed to write notes or take photographs of the records; the narrator in *Unspoken*, fearful of forgetting the potential matches she had found in the records, took to disappearing into the toilets to write these names on scraps of paper, which she then hid in her clothes.

The office is a more welcoming place today, with a dedicated search room in Werburgh Street and staff well versed in dealing with adoption queries.

I didn't have much to go on. Based on what Olive had told

staff in the hospital where I was born, Vincent Duffy was twenty-six at the time of my birth, hailed from County Monaghan and was working as a garda.

Assuming he was born in 1937, I began my search in the volume for that year. Excitingly, it contained an entry for Vincent Duffy. However, he was born in south Dublin, not the rural area I was seeking.

I widened my search to cover other years. This turned up three Vincent Duffys, the best match being a man born in 1935. There were also a few Duffys where V, possibly Vincent, was the middle initial.

In the weeks that followed, I chased these leads. In most cases, by tracking down family members, I was able to determine that the names I had listed were not relevant to my search. None of the names I had gathered fitted.

I tried other routes to track down Vincent Duffy. Olive had referred to him working in southern England as an industrial psychologist in the late 1960s. I worked my way through the English phone books, and searched death notices, but with no success. An inquiry to the professional body for industrial psychologists also drew a blank.

My next stop was the Garda Síochána museum and archives in Dublin Castle, which holds details of the service records of all past and present members of the force. Sadly, a sign on the door informed me that the museum was closed 'for the foreseeable future'. Genetically, I might be the son of a garda, but my own career as a detective was not going well.

41

As the political debate on birth information played out, the number of new adoptions dwindled to a trickle. In 1956, almost half of all non-marital births resulted in adoption; a decade later, nearly every non-marital birth ended this way. Then came the introduction of abortion in Britain in 1968, the unmarried mother's allowance in Ireland in 1973 and the abolition of the status of illegitimacy in Ireland in 1987.

By 2016, just 0.4 per cent of births outside marriage resulted in adoption. Just as in Olive's day, Irish women with crisis pregnancies flocked to Britain – but for abortions, not to place their babies for adoption.

It wasn't just that there were new options to replace adoption; public attitudes had also changed. Adoption was no longer viewed as a convenient option for hiding the shame traditionally attached to extra-marital birth, or a generous act by married couples taking in other people's children. 'Suddenly [the late 1970s and early 1980s], there was a lot of discrimination against mothers who did give up their children for adoption – people would say that they were being unfair, unkind, or weak,' social worker Laetitia Lefroy wrote in a 2024 AAI report on domestic adoption.

'Today,' UCD academics Angela Palmer and Valerie O'Brien observed in a 2018 journal article, 'it is generally more frowned upon if a parent chooses to place a child for adoption rather than if he or she rears the child as a single parent or unmarried couple.'

As a result, traditional 'stranger adoption' started to die out. There was still huge demand for children from childless couples, so foreign adoptions thrived for a while. Soon, though, they began to go out of favour or became too difficult to organise as regulations were tightened.

While children were still being placed for adoption, the majority of orders granted involved members of their wider family or step-parents. In many cases, adoption represented a regularisation of existing care arrangements, rather than the new placement of a child.

We adoptees, I realised, are a dying breed. In 2019, for example, just six children were placed for adoption in Ireland (outside a step- or extended family situation) – a far cry from the almost 1,500 adoptions that took place in 1967. Notwithstanding the problems around adoption, it seems a pity the numbers are in such steep decline.

Despite the growing clamour for change, government ministers continued to fret about the legal difficulties. In October

2020, Taoiseach Micheál Martin said he wanted to introduce legislation providing greater access to adoption records, but that 'unfettered access' would be difficult.

Any new law giving adopted people access to their birth information would be deemed unconstitutional if it failed to acknowledge the privacy rights of parents who did not want to be contacted, Minister for Children Roderic O'Gorman warned in January 2022. His Birth Information and Tracing Bill proposed a requirement for an information session with a social worker for birth mothers and adopted people before information was released. This would be held when adoptees were seeking records and one or other of the birth parents had declared a preference for 'no contact'.

Campaigners saw this provision as demeaning; I thought it a fairly tame requirement. It stayed part of the act that was signed into law by President Michael D. Higgins in June 2022, having been watered down further with a provision allowing the information session to take place by phone or video call.

What had previously been impossible could now be overcome through a quick phone call, no strings attached. Since the original Adoption Act was passed in 1952, the right of other people to privacy had always trumped the adopted person's right to information about their identity. Now that hierarchy of rights was upturned.

Birth information was to be provided through the Adoption Authority of Ireland (AAI) and Tusla, the child and family agency. The two state organisations were given control of the files of voluntary adoption agencies around the country. Applicants were told they had a right to full information and access to birth certificates, adoption records, birth and early-life information. A statutory contact preference register, established under the act, allowed for birth mothers, fathers and other affected people to register a preference to be contacted or not.

Among the thousands of documents passed to the Adoption Authority of Ireland was my file at Cúnamh. It wasn't available to me yet, but I could feel access to it getting closer by the day.

42

In early 2020 Covid-19 swept across the world. The new virus, first identified in China, spread from country to country like wildfire. Bewildered governments introduced the most swingeing restrictions on society ever seen in peacetime.

The Republic of Ireland reported its first case on 29 February. A fortnight later, Taoiseach Leo Varadkar announced the closure of all schools in an effort to stem the spread of the virus. By the end of March, dozens of people had died in Ireland and the government had announced a national stay-at-home order.

For many, forced to stay away from work, the pandemic led to a prolonged period of enforced idleness. As a health journalist reporting on the unfolding crisis, I was never busier. The offices of *The Irish Times* closed in mid-March when the first of our staff fell ill. I switched to home-working, and stayed there for most of the next two years.

I tracked the story closely from the start. My first article appeared in January, well before the virus officially reached Ireland. That month, I travelled to Geneva to report from the offices of the World Health Organization, which was leading the global response to the pandemic. Back in Dublin, I was present for all the seminal decisions announced by the Irish government. Most of the population was grounded, but journalists were among those given passes to travel and carry out their work. Time and again, I cycled the few kilometres from home to attend press conferences at Government Buildings, where shell-shocked ministers and public health experts would announce the latest set of restrictions on normal life. Each one was worse than the last. Outside, tumbleweed blew through Dublin's deserted city centre.

A career in journalism has given me a ringside seat – or thereabouts – to world events, but this was the biggest story in my career. Nothing on this scale, with such a profound and wide-ranging impact on all aspects of life, had happened in my lifetime.

In those first days of the pandemic, there was no knowing when or how the virus would be contained. The pace of change was dramatic. People were afraid but they were also confused. My job was to make sense of the situation to readers as it evolved.

It was also a time of mass reflection. Billions of people had their normal lives upended. The future looked more uncertain than ever. Time hung heavy for lives lived in lockdown. Inevitably, people were impelled to re-evaluate the quality of the lives they were leading. Many came to question the centrality of work, and centralised workplaces, in their lives.

Despite the shock and gloom, there were also positives from the pandemic. Great projects were devised and completed. Staff in the health service and other essential services laboured heroically. Communities came together in solidarity. Ultimately, science and medicine achieved major advances to tame Covid-19. The world muddled through.

In the free time I had, I started to rethink my own life. Work, family and the day-to-day business of survival were at its centre, but I had also been on a journey of discovery in relation to my identity. It was time to finish the job.

Just as news of the pandemic started filtering out of China, I had a chance encounter with a friend who told me how she had found a new half-brother. Through a DNA test, her family discovered that their deceased father had fathered a child years before he had married their mother. That child had been adopted and was living in England. The subsequent reunion had gone well.

For weeks after hearing my friend's story, as the virus edged ever closer, I thought about this option. I was familiar with DNA tests, and their power to unlock genetic secrets, but up to now I had spurned their use. I was suspicious about sharing genetic information with a commercial company. I worried a little that I might find out something negative about my health.

Now, with the pandemic bearing down and the world increasingly filled with dire predictions, my stance seemed overly precious. Who knew what this virus would do to me? Who knew where we were all going to be in a year's time? I decided I had little to lose and, potentially, much to gain by taking a test. Others would bake sourdough or take up sea swimming, but this would be *my* pandemic project.

Signing up online with one of the main genetics companies offering DNA testing is remarkably easy. The kit arrived in the post within days. Following the simple instructions, I spat into a small cylinder, sealed it and sent the sample off for processing. Then I quickly forgot about it.

43

By April 2020, Ireland was in lockdown. Cases of the virus began to soar. On my computer, the results of the DNA test flashed in my email inbox. A message invited me to log on to the firm's website to view the findings. On doing so, I learned I was 100 per cent Irish (later modified to 98 per cent Irish and 2 per cent Scottish). This was hardly a surprise to me. I closed the link and got back to work.

Further messages started to arrive for me via the company's online mailbox. The first was from a woman in Delaware who had noticed strong DNA connections between me and her family. Her dad was from the north-east of Ireland. Did I know more about the family link?

I did, of course. Again, there was no surprise here. Olive hails from the same area. The townland mentioned by my American correspondent sounded familiar. The woman kindly offered help if I needed it to discover more about my roots. But I already knew my birth mother; there were relatives around who could fill me in on that side of my family tree. I didn't take her up on the offer.

More messages arrived from distant relatives – second cousins and higher. Again, I was not interested. To an adopted person, unused to knowledge of or contact with direct blood relatives, the concept of a second cousin is arcane.

Then I received an automated message linking me to a woman labelled by the software as a first cousin or sibling. A sibling? I already knew my (half)-siblings on my mother's side, so this could only be from my genetic father's side. Suddenly, I was paying attention.

I contacted this woman through the messaging service provided by the testing company. I remember being keen not to sound overly curious, though I was anxious to learn more. In a breezy tone, I referred in the message to 'this DNA thingummy' having shown up a genetic link. Maybe we could get in touch and 'explore our common heritage', I suggested, tiptoeing around the exciting possibility that I was addressing a paternal sibling.

My new-found relative was friendly but understandably guarded in her response. My message was 'unexpected'. She politely asked for more details about me.

Yes, this is odd, I thought, sending such personal messages to a stranger. I had to remind myself: the evidence doesn't lie. Surely the DNA test had cut through years of unfocused searching, seemingly linking me to a biological father or uncle.

I mailed back the woman, relating what I knew of my origins. I mentioned the name of my birth mother and the putative name of my birth father.

Confusion ensued. Vincent Duffy meant nothing to her, and she had never heard of Olive. Furthermore, the geography was wrong. I understood Vincent Duffy to be from the border area – my birth mother mentioned Monaghan and Dundalk on different occasions — but this woman's family came from the west of Ireland. Perhaps the DNA wasn't so infallible after all.

Clearly perplexed, the woman offered to do 'a bit of digging'. 'Ireland was a strange place in the sixties so I'd imagine there is an untold story to be heard,' she wrote. I couldn't have agreed more.

We corresponded further during lockdown, sharing details of our respective families. I filled in my new contact on Olive's story and she told me about her background. 'Looking at our DNA profiles it appears we are related through my father's family,' she acknowledged. 'Some of the names that appear in the shared relative sections are names I recognise as my dad's cousins.'

Crucially, her father was a garda – just like 'Vincent Duffy' – as were his brothers. This could hardly be coincidence, we both thought. Though he had a different name, his age was about right vis-à-vis that of Olive, and mine. He had been stationed in Dublin around the time I was born.

Perhaps it was a coincidence that he was a late starter when it came to having children, just like me. Or maybe he wasn't, if I was his first-born child.

The simple DNA test had done what it could. Now the way to establish my paternal origin was to ask people direct questions. The woman offered to broach the issue gently with her father. After that, we might meet up, she suggested.

Though the end of my search for a birth father was in sight, there was a snag. With Covid rampaging across the country, the government had imposed restrictions limiting people travelling more than two kilometres from home. The roads had fallen eerily silent due to the traffic ban. People passed the time walking circuits around their local areas. Older people were especially vulnerable to the Covid virus. My putative father was isolating alone at home, so this was no time to be taking risks.

For now, there was no chance of me being able to meet with him, and my new-found relative was similarly restricted from visiting her father. Possible paternity was not the sort of topic to be broached with an octogenarian on the phone. We resolved to keep in touch, but we would have to bide our time before meeting.

44

Lockdown dragged on. I remained on tenterhooks. My half-sister or cousin and I chatted regularly on the phone. I sent her some family pictures, and one of the dog. She responded with photographs of her dad and his family. One was a recent photograph of her father with his surviving brother and sisters and another dated from his middle years. There was also a clipping from the mid-1960s, his photograph on the front page of a local newspaper. He looked handsome to me, dressed in a suit and wearing a skinny tie, but maybe I'm biased.

Her father is tall and slim, like me. In the photo, he and his brother have an athletic look to them, even in old age, as befits men who played hurling for many years. They do look their age in the most recent shot, their hair well receded, but stand erect and smiling for the camera.

Was there a resemblance? The woman thought so anyway. As usual, I was not used to looking for likenesses in people so I told her I was reluctant to go down that road. Privately, I was struck by my resemblance to him, and also to his brother.

'I suppose we seek and find the similarities we expect to find,' I said.

My half-sister, twenty years my junior, came across as a warm, positive woman. Though she grew up in Dublin, she has strong country roots and was thinking of moving there. We got on well, but it was hard to connect properly on a mobile phone.

Initially she thought my contact was a scam, she told me. Her name was on the genetics company's files only because her partner had bought her a DNA test as a Christmas present some years before. Having done the test, she forgot about it until news of the link to my results arrived. At least I wasn't 'a "foreign prince" looking to offload a family fortune', she joked.

In June, a new message arrived: 'I had a chat with my dad about two weeks ago. The word he used was flabbergasted! He remembers Olive but didn't really say much more yet. I'd like to give him some time to digest everything. I'm sure his mind is reliving everything from way back when.'

My excitement built; another piece of the jigsaw was falling into place. This man was a garda, he was in Dublin at the time I was conceived there, he knew my birth mother and they were the same age. The evidence pointed overwhelmingly to him being my father. With time and a little persuasion, he might be able to shed some light on the events that led to my birth.

I hope he was flabbergasted 'in a good way', I told his daughter, who might just be my half-sister. With the restrictions loosening, we talked about meeting up, but it was holiday season by then and both of us were moving around a lot.

We arranged to talk again after I had returned from holidays in August. In the middle of the month, shortly before coming back to Dublin, I emailed her again to suggest getting together within the week.

That didn't prove possible but we again discussed meeting up soon. The following week, as I was driving, I recalled our previous communication and made a mental note to contact her once I got home.

At that moment, an email notification arrived for me: 'I'm saddened to tell you that we lost our lovely dad last night,' the woman wrote.

'We are just heartbroken. I'm sorry that you never got the opportunity to meet him and learn what a fantastic man he was.'

45

I stopped the car at a lay-by, and got out for some air. Motorway traffic sped past as I walked up and down, trying to make sense of what had just happened. So near, yet so far. Odie, our dog, stood up in the boot and looked at me expectantly. 'Someone very close has just died,' I told him. 'And yet I never knew him.'

I thought back to the miscarriages we had experienced. It was the closest comparison I could draw on. I never got to know any of the small unborn children my wife and I lost – never touched or got to hold them. And yet we felt bereft when they died. Which was how, by the noisy, relentless motorway, I felt now.

It was the experience of witnessing my own son at play at age two and a half that triggered my search for a birth father, and for my foster mother. How right it was to be in the room with my son at that moment. How infinitely sad it was that I'd had no father to listen to my nursery rhymes at that age.

It wasn't that I wanted to blame my father for his absence in my life. History, economics, context – I got all that. Sexual urges, even. But I wanted him to know what he had missed, in me, his grandson and his granddaughters.

Too late now, I thought, on this quiet workday, six months into the Covid-19 pandemic. An average working day in the 'new normal' for me, sitting at home in my tiny office. The day of my father's funeral.

The first wave of virus cases had passed, but another wave was on the way. Many restrictions remained in place. People were still required to work at home, practise social distancing and travel no more than a few kilometres from their house. Not even for a burial.

Mid-morning, my daughter Ella brought me a cup of peppermint tea. It was time to put work aside in order to watch the funeral of the father I never met.

Modern technology makes this kind of thing possible. The pandemic and government lockdowns dictated that the funeral take place online. But nothing can tell you how you are supposed to feel in such a situation. Can you miss a father you have never known, never even seen?

I tuned in to the broadcast just as the service began. Mourners filed in to the solid, suburban church located in a prosperous city suburb. This house of God looked a lot like the one I attended growing up on the other side of Dublin. A bit less of a barn, maybe; a bit more upmarket.

I had considered attending the funeral in person – damn

the restrictions. I imagined being stopped at a checkpoint and asked by a garda why I was outside my permitted area, and replying smugly: 'Actually, I'm attending my father's funeral.' I fantasised about slipping in quietly at the back of the church just as the funeral was getting under way, and leaving just as silently before the coffin was taken out. Maybe, in proper cinematic style, my black-clad figure would hover mysteriously at the back of the cemetery, at a remove from the throng of weeping mourners, as my father's remains were being interred. Then, just as the crowd started to speculate about the unknown mourner, I would vanish.

All this sounded good in theory, but in the end I felt my attendance would not have been appropriate. It wasn't to be. In normal times it would have been perfectly possible to sit in a full church, silent and unobserved. But with lockdown rules restricting attendances to just twenty-five mourners, a stranger would inevitably stick out. I might have been drawn into expressing condolences to the family along with the other mourners, telling my siblings how sorry I was for their trouble, blushing as I concocted some cock-and-bull story to justify my presence.

The altar of the church was bedecked with late-summer flowers. The congregation, dressed heavily for the season, filed in via the central aisle. With the camera located at the back of the church, probably up near the organ, all I could see were rear profiles. The figures looked small and grainy at this remove.

There they were, my adult brother and sisters, lined up in the front row reserved for family, my father's wooden casket and their mother beside them. Strangers to me.

The priest knew the deceased, and recalled a hurling match they had both played half a century before. Each time he called up my siblings to say prayers for the faithful or read passages from the Bible, I tried to zoom the video closer on them. They were tall, and in the middle of life, I could see, but the images remained frustratingly indistinct. The game of spotting family resemblances would have to wait for another day.

The priest asked family members to place favourite objects or symbolic tokens on the coffin. Someone came up with a garda cap, in honour of a career spent in the force. Next was a county flag, though the deceased had left home early and lived most of his adult life in Dublin. A hurley followed, in tribute to his, and his county's, sporting passion. A copy of the *Irish Independent* was placed on the coffin, 'because he read it every day of his life'. As a longtime employee of the rival *Irish Times*, I got a laugh out of that one.

While the attendance lined up for Communion, I searched the internet for crumbs of information about my father. Online condolences paid tribute to a gentleman, a keen daily dog walker, a gentle soul, a family pillar and a devoted husband and dad, who was never more thrilled than when his county lifted the Liam MacCarthy Cup as All-Ireland hurling champions.

There were tributes from neighbours in Dublin and from friends who grew up with him down the country. One friend recalled sharing digs with him in a particular provincial town years before, a nugget of information that seemed to tally with something Olive had once said.

In no time, the Mass was over. A woman in a long dress and dark jacket – his elder daughter – delivered the eulogy, remaining composed despite her grief.

Her father was a garda for thirty-five years, a loving husband and a family man, she told the minuscule congregation. He lived for his county roots, the hurling, a daily read of the paper, kitchen-table chats with his children. The end had come quickly, in a private hospital three days earlier, with his children – the children who knew him – around his bed.

Sitting before my laptop, I tried on various emotions for size. Envy. Resentment. Shock. Anger. None felt right. What beef could I generate against these evidently decent people mourning the death of a loved one? What grievances could I sustain against a father I had never met?

It was one thing to rail generally about the cruel absence of men from the narrative around unmarried women who became pregnant; it was altogether something else to point a finger at a specific man. Anyway, the evidence pointed to him not knowing of my existence at the time of my birth. I was, after all, surprised to find he was still alive when I first traced him through the genetic test.

The service ended with the usual formula of obsequies. After a brief burst of applause, the mourners filed out behind the coffin. I sat looking at the image of an empty church.

Because of the pandemic restrictions, there would be no socialising outside. The transmission cut out soon after and I returned to my work, writing about Covid-19.

In the days that followed, I attempted to make sense of it all. But there was no sense to be had. What was that dad of mine but a scrap of genetic material that contributed to my make-up; part-determinant of my dimensions, physical attributes and prospective lifespan, barring accidents.

Did he write with his left hand, as I do, I wondered. Did he have a reversible thumb? Were his middle toes longer than the big ones? Had he freckles as a child? Was he argumentative, financially insecure, fascinated by politics?

It was too late for all these questions. I didn't know what he thought or how he was, and now I would never know. Yet my experience persuaded me that nurture was stronger than nature. The dad I never knew, along with Olive, helped provide the basic circuit board from which my appearance and personality developed. However, the components that really defined me were plugged in during my youth.

I could not justly complain about the absence of a birth father in my life when I already had a father, one who did everything he could to give me a good start in life. Patrick, though he bowed out of my life too early, was patient and present, everything a good father should be. He was there when he most needed to be, and everything he did in the second half of his life was for my benefit. Though not equipped with the emotional tools to express affection, not in the performative sense of hugging and kissing or even telling a person he loved them, I never sensed anything other than an all-embracing, life-affirming attachment to me, his adopted son. Could my genetic father have topped that? Let that family have their father; I had mine.

46

2022

In the years after my accident, my severe back pain episodes became less frequent. The counsel of clever physiotherapists saved me from chronic pain and a reliance on drugs to treat it. Pain is in the brain, not the spine, they showed me, and it isn't always the result of an injury. Serious back pain and tissue damage is rare, and movement can often help. A mix of stretching, relaxation and positive thinking has helped me prevent – or at least minimise – flare-ups.

It is perhaps fanciful to link physical improvements to my new willingness to investigate the past. Yet it felt good to be making progress around the circumstances of my adoption. First, there was the catharsis of meeting my birth mother and her family and then – propelled by this, the birth of my own children and a series of life challenges – the absorbing search for details of my own past in two countries.

In Ireland, my requests for information were largely rejected. But different rules applied in England, where I was born, and I had managed to obtain some records from my adoption agency in London. That in turn helped uncover more vital information. And then I had traced my birth father using a DNA test.

In October 2022, thanks to changes in the law, the day finally came when I and thousands of adopted people were entitled to access our birth information in Ireland. The logjam was broken, or so it seemed.

Well over 100,000 unmarried women had had children adopted since the Irish state was founded in 1922, so the potential take-up of the law was huge. Obviously, though, many of these people would be dead. The Adoption Authority of Ireland said it had 49,000 paper files on legal adoptions.

Adopted people applying for information were to be provided with it within months, officials promised as the new arrangements were launched. Extra staff were hired to handle the expected flow of requests.

Within days of the service opening, I made my online application to the AAI, since it now possessed my files. I asked for my file in old-fashioned hard copy, rather than electronic format.

Early optimism around the launch of the service was quickly punctured. I wanted to access the original documents in my files, but my request was rejected. The official was polite but no reasons were given.

I could understand the practical reasons for this approach, given the volume of applications the authority was receiving. But it wasn't much different from the stance taken by my adoption agency when it refused the same request I had made for access to original documents years earlier. Could the actual file be made available later, when the initial demand died down?

Promises of a quick turnaround of the files were not fulfilled. After a month, the authority wrote to say it would respond to my application 'as soon as possible' but could not meet the first, thirty-day deadline stipulated in the legislation.

By December 2022, a later, ninety-day deadline was approaching. The authority said it would not be able to meet this deadline either, due to 'an enormous quantity of applications for information'. Worse, it said the backlog would not be cleared until the following autumn, almost a year after the service opened, because of the 'unprecedented level' of applications. At that point, the authority had 2,500 applications on hand. I was going to have to wait.

It had taken decades of determined lobbying by adopted people and their supporters to get the law changed. I had watched this campaign unfold as a spectator, curiously detached from it all. My approach was a hangover from the long years when I had shown no interest in my adoption; when I was acting out the role of a 'good' adoptee. Initially, too, I believed there was no chance of my files being made available. And maybe I was being blasé, given I already knew some of the facts of my birth, including the identity of my birth mother.

My attitude had changed as the years passed, as I encountered the gaps in my birth story. Now I desperately wanted detail.

So I waited for the arrival of my documents from the Adoption Authority of Ireland with rising anticipation. I tried to limit my expectations, telling myself they were unlikely to yield any blockbuster revelations – information about my birth father, for example. I was certain, though, that more surprises were on the way.

47

2023

Another busy morning: twenty lengths in the pool before taking the bike to the train station. My back is still behaving itself. In fact, it seldom gives me serious trouble these days. How lucky I am.

I am late for the train; I need to hurry up. About to leave the house by the basement, I hear a thud, the sound of post arriving upstairs. Probably some report or book I ordered. I push out through the front door.

The package is still there when I return in the evening. Breaking it open, I find it contains three more envelopes, each one filled with copies of documents dating back decades. After a wait of over six months, my adoption file has arrived.

Here it is, my life set out on grainy sheets of A4, information that was kept secret for decades. I give the bundle an uncertain squeeze, running my hands over the smooth pages. Reading the information there and then, at the end of a long, tiring day, doesn't feel right, so I throw the package onto my work desk. I will deal with it when the moment is right, when I can give its contents the attention they deserve.

The bundle rests there for days, and then weeks. In my busy life, there is never the proper moment to read through the file carefully, without distractions. I reassure myself: to delay a pleasure is to magnify it.

Finally, on a day off work, with no-one else in the house, I make myself a cup of tea and sit down with the envelopes. I have learned from online chat forums how other adoptees fared with the release of their files. Some drew blanks. Some professed disappointment with the lack of information in their file. Many were content with details confirming what they mostly already knew. A few received surprises, even shocks. What becomes known cannot be unknown.

A cover letter from the Adoption Authority of Ireland warns of 'language or descriptions of events that some may find offensive or distressing and may contain inaccurate or false information. This is especially applicable to early records, which may contain outdated or objectionable terminology'.

A trigger warning, how very modern. Against those early years of chaos and uncertainty, an official in some office fretting about the potential impact of a few strong words seems nugatory. How could I possibly be fazed by these documents, given the insulting references about myself I have already seen? If anyone has made disrespectful comments, I am prepared to cut them some slack.

I am more concerned to find that the files relate only

to the period of my lifespan. According to the cover letter, correspondence dated from before birth and after I turned eighteen was 'not automatically released'.

I struggle to understand these restrictions. Access to files dating from before I was born might help me understand why Olive placed me for adoption. I might just be able to form a view on how much coercion was involved, and why she ended up with me in a mother and baby home.

I knew that after becoming pregnant in Ireland, she fled to England, though she had few contacts there. It must have been a terrible time to flee with a lonely secret. The winter of 1962–1963 was the coldest in over 200 years across Europe. In Ireland, a freeze set in over Christmas and 45 centimetres of snow fell on New Year's Eve. Stout, it was reported, froze in Dublin pubs as the country experienced its coldest ever January. The freeze lasted well into March on both sides of the Irish Sea.

Olive didn't tell my birth father or her family about the pregnancy. Was it possible she told no-one of her lonely predicament before I emerged into the world? How much 'encouragement' was applied before her decision to place me for adoption?

Knowing her, I think it likely that she kept the secret to herself while she was still in Ireland. However, she had to have confided in officials at the agencies in London and then Dublin in order to begin the process of having me adopted. Often a priest was the first point of contact for a young woman with a crisis pregnancy.

I empty the contents of the envelopes onto the table and flick quickly through the documents. Lines and entire paragraphs are obscured by ugly black blocks of ink. So much for getting full records. According to the cover letter, these redactions are required under data protection rules to safeguard the rights of others.

So I appeal the decision to withhold the redacted information. In particular, I ask to see records pre-dating my birth and post-dating my eighteenth birthday, to which I was refused access. I send on my adoptive parents' death certificates as evidence that they are no longer alive.

An official agrees to the release of records post my eighteenth birthday. Disappointingly, he won't provide me with any pre-birth records.

Again, I forget about the application and get on with life. The decision on my appeal arrives in my email inbox several months later. Although more records are being released to me, the adjudicating official says, some will still be redacted. Medical information about a genetic relative may not be released, 'unless it is heritable', he explains. As for inheritable genetic medical information, this can be released only to a doctor. Once again, it feels like adoptees are not to be trusted with complete information.

I look over these new records quickly on my phone one evening, not expecting any great revelations. I am wrong; even on a quick read, there are fresh surprises.

48

To read these documents – the ones I got originally, and on appeal, and on a second appeal I made – is to go back in time, and to see the world through the eyes of officials who recorded every way-station on my adoption journey. Thanks to their bureaucratic diligence – assuming it is accurate – I piece together much of that journey as I leaf through the pages one evening, after the house has fallen quiet.

I read the documents several times to make sure I do not miss important new details. As I already knew, my 'putative father' was named by Olive as Vincent Duffy, aged twenty-six, from County Monaghan. On the forms she was required to fill after my birth to start the adoption process, she listed his profession as 'policeman'. In reply to a question asking whether he had admitted paternity or offered any assistance, Olive said flatly: 'I didn't tell him.' It appears my birth father was kept in the dark about my existence.

The documents show how undecided she was about placing me for adoption. Sometimes, she appeared set on the idea; in other letters she sounded doubtful. Father Gabriel Colleran, chaplain of the CPRSI, tried to nudge her towards parting with her child.

Just after I was born and placed in foster care in England, Olive had to leave London; her nursing agency sent her to Oxford, 100 kilometres away. 'It wasn't easy to go and leave him for five weeks, [then] only seeing him once, but I wasn't able to get a job locally,' she told the priest. 'But when I came to Ireland with him I was questioned by the adoption workers as to why I left him in London and went away. I'm sure I wasn't able or ready to give them the true answer.'

It was clear from this that I saw little of Olive after we left the mother and baby home and I was in unknown private foster care arrangements. Staff at the adoption agency judged her negatively for her actions and Father Colleran issued a mild rebuke. 'Leaving a baby with foster parents is not a solution as the baby very quickly grows to love the foster parents and depend completely on them,' he told her. 'Eventually you get a tug-of-war situation and the child is the innocent sufferer.' His words turned out to be prescient.

At birth, documents record my blue eyes, my fair skin, my dark hair and my size – 'a big baby' – before throwing in a few distinctly non-medical judgements. 'Very boyish – rather coarse features,' one doctor bluntly concluded.

Parts are hard to read. Staff at the adoption agency in

London pleaded with their counterparts in Dublin to accept me, despite the medical issue, 'as we are so desperately short of nursery placements'.

Dublin wrote back to say it had no foster home available but was willing to offer me a place in a mother and baby home if Olive was willing to go there.

'Like yourselves we have not an inch of space with Foster Mothers at the moment,' a social worker said. 'We are willing to accept this child but we cannot offer an immediate foster home placement. We wonder therefore would the Mother be willing to return to St Patrick's Home for a short time (four weeks approximately) until we have a vacancy with a Foster Mother.'

A former workhouse for the poor on the Navan Road in Dublin, St Patrick's was the largest mother and baby home in the state and one of the harshest. Back in 1922, its infant mortality rate reached 50 per cent. From the 1950s on, hundreds of babies born in St Patrick's were sent to the US for adoption. In 1962, not long before it was suggested to Olive that she go there, 85 mothers and 154 children were staying in the home. Many of the referrals came from the CPRSI and the average stay for mothers was seven to nine months.

Perhaps Olive was aware of the harsh reputation of St Patrick's. Owing to my medical issue, the two of us might have ended up spending even longer in the home than was being suggested. Or perhaps she just wanted to get back to work. Unlike many younger unmarried mothers, she had a profession.

A long stay in a mother and baby home would deprive her of the ability to earn a living. To avoid this happening, Olive discharged herself prematurely from St Pelagia's.

We left after little more than a month in the home, the file baldly notes. 'I went to an apartment taking you with me,' she told me in a letter written decades later. In fact, I was placed with a private foster mother in Muswell Hill, north London, while Olive boarded nearby. Later records from Ireland show I put on considerable weight at this time, possibly the result of excessive bottle-feeding.

What drove Olive to take such a radical step, one that required her to foot the bill for my care, I wonder. To pay for my upkeep, she had to work, and by working, the bond with me was inevitably weakened. 'I would love to have kept you but found [it] nearly impossible as I had to go to work,' she told me in that later letter.

The adoption process trundled on, with more forms to complete. By the time I was two months old, I had spent time in a hospital, a mother and baby home and at least two foster care arrangements.

If the humans in this story can sometimes be unreliable narrators, so too can my adoption file. That at least is my suspicion. The file is strong on medical details, but has less to say about Olive's state of mind; in particular, her willingness or not to relinquish me.

When the adoption agency in London called to tell her that the doctor had completed my medical form, she rang off abruptly 'after trying to argue the child has not got [a] hole in his heart', according to a hand-written note on the file that points to her high level of distress.

Olive felt the need to write a contrite apology to Canon Harvey, administrator of the Crusade of Rescue, saying she had been 'most ungrateful'.

'So sorry to have put down the phone but I was a bit upset at the time,' she told the priest. 'What I meant about his heart is that seeing it is not so bad he'd be better off adopted than stuck in a nursery in Dublin for three months. As it is, he is with a foster mother and I feed him twice daily as I live a stone's throw away.'

So while Olive was not caring directly for me at this time, she was nearby. She kept up the maternal bond by feeding me daily, tending to my needs as best she could. I felt moved by this small detail. How conflicted she must have felt, going through the fundamentals of mothering while knowing that I was destined for adoption. And that, although she could theoretically shout 'stop', she, like so many other single mothers at the time, never would. What kind of emotional turmoil must that have provoked within her?

Ultimately, she gave her initial consent to the adoption. The social workers in Dublin got a foster home available. They asked Canon Harvey to send Olive 'whenever it is convenient'. I was about to come to Ireland.

49

On 7 October 1963, precisely fifty-four years before I fall off a mountain in Germany, I am bundled onto a London evening train bound for Liverpool, to be repatriated to Dublin via the night ferry. My birth mother foots the cost of this grim journey.

She has been given her travel instructions: 'Must travel by 4.50 p.m. train – Euston – to North Wall via Liverpool. Mrs Murphy to meet her. Not to travel during last week of September.'

Mrs Murphy, otherwise known as 'Murphs', had by then escorted scores of mothers and their babies on the final leg of their journey from the UK to Ireland. She began working for the CPRSI in 1931 and continued in this lonely job until her death in 1977. 'She was the sole [sic] of discretion and played a vital role in the work of repatriation,' a colleague recalled, decades later, in the Cúnamh book, *All Born Under the One Blue Sky*.

Money, as ever, figures prominently for the adoption agencies. 'I take it for granted she [Olive] pays her own fare. We would if she could not manage,' staff in London tell their counterparts in Dublin.

Olive arrives in Dublin Port as arranged in the early morning and is met by Mrs Murphy. From here, the adoption agency assumes responsibility for my care.

The following day Olive signs a consent to place her five-month-old son in 'temporary' foster care. She agrees to pay £2 a week (almost €50 in today's terms) towards my upkeep.

By now I weigh 15 pounds, 11 ounces (7.1 kilograms) and am fully weaned. Although I am marked as having heart disease that has to be treated, my murmur is noted as being 'of no obvious significance clinically'. And yet it will delay my official adoption for three years.

The agency repeatedly presses Olive to contribute to my upkeep. This is despite its later claim that it sought contributions only in 'exceptional circumstances and in appropriate instances'. When she can, she encloses cheques for me with her letters to social workers. Sometimes, she sends baby clothes.

I had been reading the file for several hours before I came across a reference to my foster care in Ireland. There had been several short-term foster mothers in London while Olive was out working, but this was different. The woman referred to as F.M. in the documents was likely to have played a central role in my upbringing from this point. I was keen to learn more. Going to bed could wait.

My foster mother was paid £7 a month for caring for me, 'not by way of reward', her agreement with the agency stated. She was to provide the 'moral training, physical comfort and supervision that the child has been deprived of through the loss of his own home'. I was expected to have my own bed, and she was to be 'interested in and report on [my] progress and behaviour'.

The amount paid to her was less than the £2 a week Olive was required to remit in return for my being cared for 'and brought up a Catholic' by the adoption agency. My care was effectively cost-neutral for the agency.

Olive continued to struggle financially while I was in foster care. She also grew frustrated at the delays in placing me for adoption. She told the adoption agency she knew the name of a doctor in England 'who does adoptions on the side' and suggested he might be able to help them place me. Sending clothes once again, Olive apologised for having no money to send. She did send another £10 a few months later but asked if I could be adopted soon because 'I can't keep up with the account'. Her options were clearly narrowing.

I passed my first birthday still in foster care. There is no indication in the file that it was marked in any way. Given I clearly remember my oldest daughter's first birthday and that was almost twenty years earlier, I couldn't help feeling sad about this small omission.

In January 1965 – when I was nineteen months old – Olive told the priest 'adoption is the best solution'. But time and again, for some reason, she put off giving a final yes.

Six months later, she was back in Father Colleran's office. 'Finding it very difficult to make a decision – just will not face up to it,' the priest recorded in his notes. She told him her only hope of hanging on to me rested on a married sister in Dublin, who remained in the dark about her pregnancy and birth. 'Not much of a chance' that she would tell her sister, Father Colleran guessed.

Olive's turmoil grew. She 'seemed to be very much on edge – played nervously with her gloves all the time and became very vacant at intervals', the priest noted at their next meeting.

As he predicted, she did not tell her sister. The adoption went through.

A separate cache of documents from the Adoption Board tracked my parents' application to adopt me, from the investigations made of them to my adoption order. My adoption was delayed for years over health issues and the doubts Olive had about giving me up. Even so, the board moved slowly. By the time it got around to listing my case for hearing, I was three years old, and had been living with Mary and Pat for months.

The file recorded my parents' anxieties during this interregnum, while my adoption remained incomplete. Mary and

Pat 'keep on being apprehensive and refuse to be reassured pending hearing', staff noted.

On the day of the hearing, at the board's offices on St Stephen's Green in Dublin, my parents were required to testify in person in support of their application – no doubt a daunting experience.

Fortunately, they had been favourably reviewed by officials. The board's investigator said they appeared to be 'very reliable people' with a 'kindly, quiet disposition' and a 'tidy, happy home'. 'They are inclined to be anxious about finalising the application,' he noted. 'They had hoped for their own children' – the middle of the sentence is redacted – 'decided to start a family by adoption.'

The investigator said that my parents' home was in 'very good condition – well-equipped – comfortable', located near a church, under construction, and schools.

As for me, I was considered 'a grand little boy – strong, healthy, reasonably well adjusted. He is of a happy nature, very bright, mature for his age,' the investigator concluded.

My parents supplied a reference from their priest describing them as 'excellent Catholics' who could offer 'a nice home to an adopted child'. The Garda Síochána said nothing had been shown in their records against my parents 'in relation to honesty, sobriety or moral character or of conviction for an offence'.

The form listed my father's occupation as a painter. My mother wasn't asked for hers.

The consent form for my adoption was filled out by officials in London, with Olive supplying her signature there in a heavy hand. She was required to swear her religion, and my name and birth-date, on oath, and to attest that 'I did not marry the father of my child'.

Finally, she surrendered all her parental rights with the following oath: 'I understand that the effect of an adoption order is to deprive me of all rights which I have in respect of the upbringing of the child, and to give these rights and all parental rights and duties to the adopter.'

From this point on, there was no going back.

50

I took another break from reading the file in the quiet of my kitchen. So used was I to reading official documents for work, I had to pinch myself. This was not some report or press release that I was reading as a journalist, with a view to writing it up as an article. These words related to *me*.

The file served up a less flattering account of my adoption agency than emerged from the limited material it previously had provided to me. Staff could be quick to pass judgement, despite the often desperate circumstances of the women and children going through their services. They frequently expressed themselves in a manner that was both insulting and ignorant.

For example, an unsigned, handwritten note on one letter described Olive, who had just taken the overnight boat-train from London and was about to relinquish her first-born child, as an 'untidy, casual type'. As for five-month-old me, I was dismissed as 'huge, really gross'.

Later, after I was placed with my foster mother, Olive and I were briefly reunited at a meeting in the offices of the adoption agency. My birth mother thought I looked 'too fat'. A censorious adoption worker jumped to the conclusion that she 'had not a clue about holding' me, causing me to cry 'all the time'. Later that day, however, it emerged that I had been developing chickenpox – the real reason for my tears.

There is a revealing exchange between my social worker and Father Colleran, written on the margins of a letter from my adoptive parents in which they begged to be allowed to adopt a second child.

In 1969, Mam called into the agency and asked why she had been 'put off' adopting a second baby. Asked her age, she claimed she was 'over forty-six' while Dad was 'about fifty'. This was, admittedly, a fib. They were both at least three years older then – too old to adopt.

Dad followed up with a letter in which he highlighted the 'great success' they had made of adopting me but pointed out that I 'would be very much alone in the world without some other member of his little family'.

'I would have applied soon after we adopted Paul but it took a long time to settle the boy down as he was 2½ when I got him and was termed a difficult child. We are quite capable of rearing even more than two as we both come from and understand large families.'

Father Colleran scribbled a note to the social worker asking 'Is this yours?', to which she replied: 'Would you answer this awful woman – my patience wouldn't hold out! I'm tired writing and talking to her.'

The emollient priest told my parents that the destiny of the fourteen-month-old girl they were hoping to adopt had been 'decided upon'. She was now with other adoptive parents.

Olive never forgot or stopped worrying about me. With heartbreaking regularity, after I was formally adopted and she had no more contact with me, her letters arrived at the adoption agency seeking updates on my condition. As the years passed, and her troubles mounted, the letters grew longer and more reflective. She confided in Father Colleran regularly. He sought to allay her fears.

The agency also tried to ease her concerns, staff telling her 'everything has worked out very well' and that I had 'settled down', even when this was not true.

But her regrets grew with the years. In one letter she asked if I was 'well-adjusted' to my adoptive parents; in another, she wondered aloud if I was clear of my 'hole-in-the-heart' condition.

In 1968, she wanted to know if there was a possibility of my parents adopting another child because I would be 'the better of a brother or sister'. Ironically, this was when Mary and Pat were trying to adopt again, but they had left it too late.

Olive's letters frequently referred to the personal problems she was facing. She spent eight months in a—' The word or words that follow are redacted from the file. But she had told me about her time in a psychiatric institution herself. She gave up nursing because it was too hard and later found work in a 'laundry'.

'Sometimes I think of him quite a lot, especially as I'm living at home and the pace is much quieter,' she said in a letter sent to Father Colleran when I was five. She said she was thinking of looking for work in a home as 'I'm fond of children'. The priest suggested that she get in touch with the mother superior at St Patrick's mother and baby home on the Navan Road in Dublin.

And so, extraordinarily, Olive, who had lived with me in a mother and baby home in London and narrowly avoided being sent to St Patrick's when she returned to Ireland, ended up working there, years after I had been adopted.

It must have been terrible for her, being surrounded by all those single mothers who had just given birth, knowing from her own bitter experience exactly what lay ahead for them after they were separated from their child.

The experience served to change her views on adoption, as well as adding to the regret she already felt for giving me up. Working in the mother and baby home, Olive saw 'lots of girls who wanted to keep their babies but had nowhere to put them to be fostered. In England most girls who are unmarried keep their babies. It's about time it spread to this country.'

There are hints in the correspondence of the pressure she was put under to relinquish me. The Crusade of Rescue, the British charity that organised my transfer back to Ireland, was 'too anxious' to get children adopted, Olive told Father Colleran.

In Ireland, too much emphasis was placed on 'the child', she complained. 'After all, the mother has to live the rest of her life also and she is already unfortunate enough to have had a baby without having to part with it.

'I know she doesn't have to part with it but what alternative is there? If [only] the Crusade of Rescue or some other organisation would try and get foster homes for girls who wanted to keep their babies and for whom it would be best to keep their babies.'

She contrasted the situation of 'well-meaning' adoptive parents with the plight of the unmarried mother who 'drifted apart from her own family and she has really nobody'. I assume she was describing her own position.

Any child can lose his father through death, she pointed out: 'So why, if the child got a decent foster home, should he not be kept by his mother? I was told when Paul was fostered out before he was adopted that I couldn't have him there if I wanted to keep him.'

Her letters to the agency continued as I grew up far away from her. In December 1970 she wrote again to Father Colleran, requesting a photo of me, and adding: 'It is not for the father of the child I want it as he has returned to England and I don't expect to see him again.'

By 1973 she was married. She had a little girl aged ten months 'but I still think of and sometimes worry about Paul'. Five years passed before she wrote again, saying she felt 'responsibility' for me and that, with luck, she would be able to look me up within three years, when I turned eighteen.

From my reading of the file, Olive had next to no choice in the decision to put me up for adoption. Notwithstanding the odd friendly voice, she came under sustained pressure to do so from English officials and the adoption agencies in London and Dublin. She fought off this pressure for a while and tried to put in place private care arrangements while she worked, but the economics of this didn't add up. She couldn't work and see me regularly at the same time.

My adoption agency has said publicly that it supported young women who wanted to keep their babies by funding foster care for them. Maybe it did, but not in my case. I was placed in a foster home, largely beyond the reach of my birth mother. My foster placement was effectively the departure lounge for adoption.

Considering these factors, I believe mine was as forced an adoption as you could get.

Perhaps Olive also came to that realisation. 'I'm delighted that times have changed now and that it is a lot easier for single parents to look after their own child. Also, it has become more acceptable,' she told me many years later in a letter.

51

More hours go by as I read the documents, becoming ever more immersed in the world of the 1960s. Then, suddenly, I see a detail I had been seeking for so long. There, at the end of a short note to the adoption agency, is the name of my foster mother, Imelda Walsh. And her address, in Bray, County Wicklow.

I grab my phone and open Google Maps. Sure enough, the road is there, part of a small estate of houses in this seaside town. A few more clicks and there before me is a photograph of the house as it is now, over half a century on from when I lived there.

Google Street View shows me a small, grey-fronted terraced dwelling with a postage-stamp front garden bounded by plain black railings. A satellite dish attached to the wall is obviously modern, as are the PVC windows, but otherwise the front of the house and the slate roof look broadly as they might have done in the 1960s. This is where I lived from the age of four months to almost two and a half years.

Obviously, I can't see into the house, and the blinds on the windows are half-down. But my mind is already running riot. I must have played in the front room below, and slept in an upstairs bedroom. I can almost see the small bed I occupied, and the modest kitchen at the back where I was fed. I am sure I must have taken my first steps on the scrap of grass I can see to the front of the house, and held on for dear life to those iron railings in the photo.

Throughout the file, my foster mother – or F.M., as she is referred to – remains an enigmatic character. In their letters, staff in the adoption agency never addressed her by her first name; she signed herself as Mrs Walsh, or sometimes Mrs I. Walsh. She was constantly doing their bidding, her tone invariably deferential. On one occasion, when she used the agency's account without authorisation to buy a play-pen, she had to apologise profusely to staff there.

This was my sole foster placement after returning to Ireland, I was relieved to discover. Research shows that multiple changes in foster care are linked with worse outcomes for an adopted person in later life. Also, I was not Mrs Walsh's first foster child, so there may have been other children for company in those early months and years. Mind you, there wouldn't have been much space for us in this little house.

Bray then was a traditional holiday resort in gentle decline, which could be reached from Dublin by bus or train. Most of my short life up to this point had been spent in London, either in hospital, a mother and baby home, private foster care or, briefly, with Olive. After these months of turbulence, my life finally became more stable. I would remain with Mrs Walsh for over two years.

I hadn't seriously considered before now that this most formative period of my life was spent not with my birth or adoptive mother, but with someone else. And now I was reading her name for the first time.

And yet there wasn't much to be learned about Mrs Walsh in the files. She put me on infant formula. She reported regularly to the agency on my progress. She brought me to multiple medical appointments. She also brought me several times to the CPRSI's office in Dublin, where I met Olive when she was home from England. It is unclear whether the two women were allowed to meet. Mrs Walsh nursed me through chickenpox, measles and pneumonia while caring for her other charges. She sent on baby pics (oh, to see them now!). She sang my praises in her letters to the agency. At the end, poignantly for me, she wrote that she would love to have kept me 'if only I could afford to'.

When I was aged fifteen months, the file records, Mrs Walsh took me to Butlin's, a holiday camp in County Meath, but was forced to come home early as I 'never stopped crying and I thought it would injure him'. That sounded alarming!

Mrs Walsh was constantly concerned for my health. Her house was frequently beset by illness. Worrying about my heart murmur, she took me to see a well-known heart specialist, Professor Conor Ward. One of the first paediatric cardiologists in Ireland, Professor Ward pioneered surgery on children with minor cardiac abnormalities. He even has a syndrome named after him. He died as recently as 2021, at the age of ninety-eight. After multiple visits and tests, he pronounced me 'perfectly normal' in June 1965, when I was two.

Olive christened me Paul. At school, I was to end up in a class full of Pauls, and many of my closest friends are called Paul. It has become something of a standing joke, this profusion of Pauls in our lives.

I had always assumed we were named for Pope Paul VI, another of the religious figures to feature on our walls when I was growing up. After all, the same thing happened again a generation later when Ireland filled up with John Pauls after the visit of the Polish-born Pope John Paul II in 1979. On checking, though, I see Pope Paul VI was elected a month *after* I was born. Whatever about my friends, I couldn't have been named after him.

Now the files revealed something odd. Paul Gerard is the full name on my birth certificate. Back during my years in foster care, at the stage when I was learning to respond to a name and say my own, I was called ... Gerard. It isn't clear why this happened, since I am always referred to as Paul in the files.

Perhaps there was another Paul in the foster home before I arrived.

When I went to live with Mary and Pat, I became Paul again. My adoption worker said she told them of my foster mother's use of Gerard, but they must have forgotten or ignored this.

It felt strange to think I might have been known as Gerard Cullen. Perhaps, with a different name, I might have followed a different path in life. But it explained somewhat the upset I endured when I was first moved to live with my adoptive parents.

52

My half-sister was friendly and welcoming as we sipped tea in her home. She was happy to talk about her father, who happens also to be my father. Shortly after his death, she had kindly agreed to meet me.

It was clear they had a deep bond and she was grieving still. She explained how she had broken the news of my contact with her as delicately as possible to her father. In doing so, she mentioned Olive and also the results of my DNA test, which indicated that the two of them were my genetic parents.

Her father remembered Olive, spoke kindly of her and even asked how she was now. But he expressed surprise when told the result of the DNA test, and what it revealed. He was taken aback at this news, she said.

Notwithstanding his surprise, he was open to meeting me. Because of his premature death, that never happened. My genetic father went to hospital for a scheduled, routine procedure. While he was there, the doctors referred him for tests. In the course of these, he fell seriously ill and died a few days later, his family around him.

*

I met my half-sister a few times after that. She came around for dinner once but then moved away from Dublin, and opportunities for meeting up diminished. She told a sister about me early on but not her brother or mother.

Further DNA tests might have established with absolute certainty that this man was my father. That wasn't possible now, due to the lack of contact, but I wasn't sure I cared anymore. I knew now that my father existed, and had a life, even if I was never going to meet him.

As in so many adoption narratives, the father is the missing element in my story. My birth father remains 'just like an elusive shadow, hovering in the background of a case', to use the description by Monsignor Cecil Barrett of 'the putative father' in his 1952 pamphlet on adoption. 'Some girls know very little about him; others are unwilling to speak about him; some say so much about him that it is difficult to know how much of it is true,' the priest wrote.

Much changed over the decades that followed, but not the elusiveness of birth fathers. Writing recently in retirement, social worker Anne Ronayne commented that she had *never* met a birth father in over forty years working in adoption.

Because of the history of near misses and broken trails, I have learned little enough about my birth father and the circumstances that brought him together with Olive. I cannot explain why there is so much seemingly false information about him in my files, though none of this is a bar on theorising.

I know he was a garda at the time he met my birth mother. Olive is clear she did not tell him – or anyone else – about the pregnancy. 'The fact is that your dad didn't actually know I was pregnant with you,' she told me once in a letter. 'I made an effort to let him know by beating around the bush but I didn't tell him.'

Beyond these basic snippets, the information I have is inconsistent. Olive gave his name as Vincent Duffy when dealing with nurses and other health staff at the time of my birth. She described him as coming from the north-east of Ireland. However, my putative birth father bears a different name. He grew up in a different part of the country.

So did Olive supply the officials with a false name for my birth father? If Vincent Duffy was a fiction, to what end? To preserve his privacy? To prevent him from tracing me? This wasn't that unusual with birth mothers trying to put the birth of a child outside marriage behind them.

Was Vincent Duffy perhaps a 'toe-tag' father? (It used to be the practice to attach an identity tag to the foot of a dead person in hospital. The name of this corpse was sometimes 'borrowed' for the fathers of children born out of wedlock, on the basis that dead men can't answer questions.)

Olive appears to have been sceptical about some of what he

told her. When my father claimed to be working in a particular garda station, Olive told a social worker the town didn't have a barracks. But could she have genuinely believed his name was Vincent Duffy? It seems unlikely, but is worth examining. It would mean he provided her with a false name, along with other incorrect personal information. The question of motive arises.

Olive was twenty-five at the time I was conceived, a grown woman with a profession. She was also a quiet person with mental health challenges. She was vulnerable and could have been taken advantage of.

Before I ever met Olive, we corresponded for a number of months through the adoption agency. I went back to these letters to see if they contained any clues about my father, and tried to marry the details in them with the file I had just received. Re-reading the letters after many years, I found Olive had given me the same information about Vincent Duffy as she had provided to the officials who arranged my adoption decades earlier. Her story hadn't changed over more than thirty years.

53

I decide to quiz Olive again. She already knows about the result of the DNA test because I told my half-sisters and they raised it with her.

Talking to her by phone, I ask what she thinks of the mother-and-baby-home report. It was published a while back but is still in the news.

There is a pause on the line before she answers. 'Mother and baby homes were not a good idea.'

The line goes quiet again. I can hear a kettle heating in the background.

'But you know about them yourself – you were in one.'

'I was. It wasn't great.'

The water has boiled now, the kettle has clicked off. More silence.

'I've traced my father, you know.'

'Aye.'

'I took one of those DNA tests. They look at your genes and match them with other people's. I've been in contact with a woman whose father seems to be my father.'

'Aye.'

'And he's *not* called Vincent Duffy.'

'Aye.'

'And he died before I could talk to him.'

No hint of a reaction on her side of the call. 'Aye. I'll say a prayer for him.'

'How come he had a different name from the one you gave me?'

'That wasn't right.'

'What wasn't right?'

'None of it was right, back then. He must have given me a false name.'

'A false name?'

'That was what they did at the time.'

'But how long did you know him?'

'A bit, I suppose.'

'Did you know anyone from his family – his brothers, for example?'

'A bit.'

'How long is a bit?'

'I don't know – a year, maybe.'

Throughout the years of our relationship, I'd had many frustrations about the blockages to finding out about my past. I'd always pushed them aside. After all, Olive's evasions were no different from the walls of secrecy erected by my adoption agency. And she was, I understood, a product of her time. Now, though, I couldn't hold back.

'Ah come on, Olive. Are you saying you knew him for a year and all that time he gave you a false name? And no-one around the two of you said anything different? Do you expect me to believe that?'

My sudden outburst, rather than opening her up, has the opposite effect.

'That's it, I suppose,' she says. 'I have people here, waiting for their tea. I have to go. Thanks for the call. Talk soon.'

I have been dropped like a hot potato. There is no coming back.

'Bye.'

'Bye.'

There is a postscript to Olive's story of her relationship with my birth father. It is set out in her letters, which I retrieved from a box I had stored years before in the attic at home.

Olive said she last saw my birth father in the late 1960s or early 1970s. By this time, I had been legally adopted and she had not seen me for over five years. She could have had little expectation of ever seeing me again.

'The last time I saw him before [this] was before you were born,' she wrote to me in one letter. 'I tried to contact him after you were born but failed. Then he turned up out of the blue when you were eight.

'I got such a shock when he rang me one day at work that I didn't ask him many questions but he found out that you were adopted. At that time the law was different and I didn't think that we'd be able to make contact with you again.'

The letter dates from before we met in person. I imagine she was keen then to be seen to be open and transparent, so that our reunion would go ahead. After we met, she was never as forthcoming. And as the years turned into decades, her memory became increasingly frail, so that it became hard to distinguish obfuscation from forgetfulness.

In this letter, she told me my birth father was working as an industrial psychologist, living in London (in another letter, she gave the location as 'the south of England'). Though this information was remarkably specific, I failed to locate any Vincent Duffy with this profession in either location.

It did occur to my father about a year after they met that I might have been conceived and born, Olive wrote in the letter. Referring to my own 'slightly grey' hair at the time, she added: 'Your dad was quite grey when he came back to visit me.'

By the time my father turned up again unexpectedly (when I was six or eight, depending on the different versions given by Olive), she was going out with her future husband. 'He said he'd come again in a year but I was married in a year after that,' she told me.

'Your dad was interested in you and I know he'd love to have seen you from the way he spoke. I'm sorry that I haven't got his address but I will try to trace him for you. I don't mind in the least the fact that you would like to make contact with him also.'

Correspondence in my file provided another insight into the lonely burden Olive carried for so long after I was adopted. When she had made contact and I, still young and living at home, had declined to meet her, she wrote to the Department of Health. Could the department not change the law to permit contact between adoptees and their birth mothers, she pleaded.

This was so unlike the stoic Olive I had come to know; she must have been suffering greatly due to my absence in her life, despite the passage of years. There was sadness and longing in her simple letter to the department, but determination too.

The response from a civil servant was polite but dismissive: 'Up to now, adoption arrangements have been subject to a great deal of confidentiality and it is probable that most persons who have been party to them would not wish to have that confidentiality breached.'

A few years later, after I had indicated a willingness to meet her, Olive was summoned to the adoption agency. 'With the passing of the years she has come to accept what happened,' the social worker's notes record, 'and when I told her about 10 years ago that he wasn't interested in having a meeting she accepted that.

'There isn't any great enthusiasm in Olwyn [sic] about

this but then Olwyn seems to be a little bit dead-pan about everything.'

Without being prompted, Olive asked the social worker whether I would be interested in finding out about my genetic father, and wondered if the agency could help find him. Again here, she said my father was Vincent Duffy, from Dundalk, adding that she knew nothing more about him. She repeated the story about being contacted by Vincent Duffy when I was eight and she was back in Ireland and working in a hospital in Navan.

A few months later, she wrote to a parish priest in Dundalk asking for help in tracking down Vincent Duffy. If the name of my father was a fiction, it was one repeated many times.

The priest passed on her request to local social workers but they were unable to help. The trail ran dry again.

The version of events around Vincent Duffy as given by Olive cannot be reconciled with the DNA evidence. My genetic father spent his entire career in the Irish police force and never worked in the UK, according to his daughter. He never met Olive again after their original encounter, he told her.

While Olive undertook to trace my birth father in the letter she sent me before we met for the first time, she declined to talk about him in any way in all further conversations I had with her over many years.

And yet there is considerable detail in her written account of meeting him when I would have been a young child living with my adoptive parents. Again, if this is a fabrication, it is a detailed one.

There is yet another possibility; that there was a Vincent Duffy, whom Olive knew and believed to be the father of her child, but who was not in fact my father. Both Vincent Duffy and my genetic father were gardaí; perhaps they were colleagues, even friends, at some point in their careers? Maybe they socialised together for a time?

Perhaps these intriguing notions belong to the realm of screenwriting more than real life; unexpected plot-twists that take the reader by surprise. And yet the torrid history of adoption in twentieth-century Ireland has thrown up many such intricate histories.

I made one last effort to solve this mystery by asking the Garda Museum in Dublin Castle, which holds the service records of all gardaí, to do a search for Vincent Duffy. The museum was now open again.

Excitingly, its search quickly threw up one Vincent Duffy who had served in the force. Unfortunately, this was a motor mechanic from County Monaghan who also fought with the old IRA and retired from policing back in 1924, long before I was born.

Further searches identified a number of other officers called Duffy with Vincent as a middle name, but they hailed from other parts of the country. My searches ran into the ground. The riddle of Vincent Duffy remains unsolved.

54

Dad has been dead for almost four decades now. His generation has all but disappeared. The mark he made upon the earth is practically expunged. I am the last person left who remembers him as a fully rounded individual. Yet even my impressions of him are fading.

Most date from the end of his life, when he was past his best. I recall a man looking and dressing older than his years, snoring gently on the patterned settee in his grey cardigan, his head thrown back and his mouth open. His paint-flecked glasses have fallen onto his lap; the unruly thatch of grey hairs projecting from his eyebrows fascinates me. Even in sleep, a worried furrow cuts his brow, as if anticipating the next disaster around the corner.

Today, coming across small keepsakes kick-starts memories. An old textbook, the metal combs he used in his trade, a broken watch in a jewellery box. All help me visualise his gentle presence. Despite the passage of time, I can see him standing before me again in his signature overalls, frayed from repeated washing, resignation written on his face, his inner thoughts a mystery to me.

The walls and windows he decorated so painstakingly have long since been painted over by others. But maybe one of the secret sketches he loved to make on a wall before decorating it survives beneath layers of fading wallpaper.

Becoming a father and raising a child was his life's project. He left behind gifts that cannot be seen or measured. Ethereal qualities: an uncomplicated goodness, a capacity for love, respect for nature. In regular families, these intangible elements are passed through the genes. In my case, as an adoptee, they were learned through instruction and simply sharing the same serene space as my father.

I think back to my teens, how hard I was on him. I was afraid of Mam, and I took it out on Dad. Curt and non-communicative, I would walk out of the room when he entered, seething at the mere sight of him dozing in front of the television, this old man, so out of touch and uncool.

I was a prat, but it didn't last.

I recall with fondness the first and last road trip we made together, shortly before Dad died. We set out for Donegal in his blue, wooden-framed Morris Minor Traveller, with me at the steering wheel on a provisional licence. We had never gone on an adventure bigger than a day-trip to a beach near Wicklow town so I was surprised that Dad had agreed to this.

He had one stipulation: I was not to go anywhere near Northern Ireland. He made me promise.

It was the mid-1980s, and the conflict in the North was

dragging on. That year, the IRA's Brighton hotel bombing nearly killed Margaret Thatcher. There were still occasional landmine explosions and shootings across the North.

I agreed to his condition, and we headed up to the north-west via Sligo. The pair of us enjoyed a perfectly lovely weekend, pottering around the sights of Donegal. We stayed in small bed and breakfasts, where Dad filled his flask with tea that he drank with our takeaway chips each evening.

On Sunday, I turned the car for home. As I drove south, the sign for Enniskillen caught my eye. On the spur of the moment, I opted to cross the border. It was quicker that way. Once in the North, I chose a back road where, I hoped, we were unlikely to run into any army patrols. I sweated a bit while Dad dozed beside me, realising I was nervous myself. The journey turned out to be uneventful.

I told him we had passed through the 'war-torn' North only when we were safely back in the Republic. He hadn't noticed a thing, having slept for most of the time we were in British territory. He recovered quickly from the shock, and there was something more. I sensed a curiosity on his part that I had never seen before, a tinge of regret that he hadn't been more adventurous in life.

We talked about taking more trips down the country, maybe even putting the car on the ferry to Britain or France. But that was to be our last trip together. Short months later, he was gone from us.

55

Mary and Pat were products of a different time. They came from big families and impoverished backgrounds, and grew up in a state that failed them educationally and economically. Mam suffered major disappointments growing up and then the crushing loss of her first, unborn child in brutal circumstances. Not only that, but she lost the ability to conceive more children. She lived with a keen sense of what might have been, had she received a proper education and a better roll of the dice. She had drive and ambition, but never got the chance to use them.

Dad, though shy and stay-at-home by nature, was forced to emigrate repeatedly to make ends meet. He built up a business and then suffered its collapse, leaving him ruined financially and scarred psychologically. The experience destroyed his confidence for the rest of his life. The loss of their child must also have affected him, though men didn't talk about those things back then.

Certainly, Mam and Dad weren't the only ones to endure such hardship. Had my father been born almost anywhere else in Europe, he would have ended up as cannon fodder in a world war. But my parents never learned to deal with the adversity they had suffered, let alone overcome it. The support services we take for granted today were barely in existence when they most needed them.

That is their story, growing up in inner-city Dublin. Things were no better in rural Ireland, where Olive was reared just a few years after them.

Raised by an emotionally distant father after her mother died prematurely, my birth mother suffered even greater adversity than my adoptive parents. Though quiet and withdrawn, she had to work hard from an early age, before she was able to cope. Scarred by the harrowing experience of working in a mental asylum as a very young woman, at a time when Ireland was locking up more psychiatric patients than any other country, she went on to suffer mental health problems herself. The treatment she was administered, which included electric shock therapy, is today regarded as barbaric. Like Patrick, she was forced by economic necessity to leave Ireland repeatedly for work; the resulting isolation only added to her problems. Although she married eventually, she was a damaged person by this time.

And then there was me. Olive doesn't talk about her feelings when I was conceived and born. The files offer few glimpses into her state of mind back then.

But these are the facts: she told no-one about her pregnancy, including my father, presumably out of shame or a fear of retribution. She was forced to leave Ireland in order to hide it. To make ends meet, she had to work long hours, often on the night shift, while carrying a first child. She spent time in a harsh mother and baby home after giving birth to me in a foreign city where she knew no-one. She was forced to place me in private foster care because she was unable to mind me while working and was unable to support me when she wasn't. She was even sent to work in another city while I was being fostered, because that was the only place where employment was available.

As she told me in a letter many years ago, 'I would prefer to have been able to care for you myself and bring you up but I had to work and I had nobody to help me. I kept you for almost six months but finding suitable carers was nearly impossible.'

None of the social services or agencies she dealt with helped her in any way to provide for her own child. Her welfare did not figure highly in any of their agendas. The main objective of British social services was that she return to Ireland with her baby as quickly as possible, so we would not be a drain on their resources. The two adoption agencies she dealt with in London and Dublin had little enough interest in her welfare. They were set up to ensure that umarried women had their babies adopted by Catholic families – and so were not lost to Protestants.

Going on the limited records available to me, neither agency explicitly demanded that I be put up for adoption. However, they did the next best thing, by removing all other options for her. The agencies never missed an opportunity to extract a financial price for their services, even making my birth mother pay for the ferry trip home with me.

In Ireland, social workers placed me in foster care for over two years as a prelude to adoption but they never contemplated making this option available to Olive as a single mother. To do so would not have cost my adoption agency anything extra, but it didn't suit the national agenda at the time.

Olive, struggling financially and making decisions in isolation, procrastinated about placing me for adoption. This didn't bother the agency too much at first because I had to be passed as medically fit in order to be placed and my heart needed to be checked out.

Once I got the all-clear from the doctors, the social workers in Dublin ramped up the pressure on Olive to sign the necessary papers. When the social workers couldn't get her approval, my reading of the files tells me, they brought in the big guns, in the form of their Catholic chaplain. And all the time the agency was making a paper profit on my fosterage by charging Olive more for my keep than it was paying my foster mother.

It was only much later, after she had witnessed the workings of a mother and baby home first-hand by working in one, that Olive learned to articulate her concerns. Long after she could do anything about it, she realised there could have been another way. By then it was too late for her, because I had been legally and irreversibly adopted.

56

On a fine Sunday afternoon in autumn 2023, I find myself standing outside the house in Bray where I lived as a small child for two years. Once home to the woman for whom I have long searched – Mrs Walsh – who cared for me after my mother reluctantly gave me up, and before I was adopted by my parents. The missing piece of the jigsaw.

I live so close by that I have cycled here. Tarrying on the road, I pick up a faint scent of sea in the air, though the house, deep in the town, is well away from the beach.

In the National Library, I tracked down a short article in a local newspaper marking Mrs Walsh's death at the age of eighty-one. From London, she lived in Bray for most of her life. 'A friendly, good-humoured lady, she was well-known and very popular. She had been in poor health for some time but always kept the best side out,' according to the appreciation.

She had no family of her own but looked after sixteen children over the years and adopted three boys. 'She loved children and gave of her very best in keeping them happy and contented,' the article said.

I'm not sure what I expect to find in coming here. I suppose I am on a pilgrimage of hope.

I pace up and down the pavement, taking a few photos. No doubt I look suspicious, just hanging around like this – except for the cycling shorts. Finally, I gather my courage and walk up the driveway. For a while after I knock, nothing happens. Then I hear the sound of a television being turned down. A man opens the door cautiously. I explain the rather bizarre reason for my visit.

The man isn't connected to Mrs Walsh or her family, but he has heard of her. He kindly asks me in. His wife and adult son are at home, and he introduces me to them. I explain my link to the house once again, and they bid me to sit down while tea is made. I sit on the couch in their small front room, as I had, presumably, more than half a century earlier. I am back where I started, where I pottered around as a toddler, where I ate my first solids. Where my brain grew to three-quarters of its adult weight, and I added one million synapses a second. Where I was potty-trained and was taught my first words. It feels like a circle is being closed.

My host confirms that Mrs Walsh is long dead, but she might still have family in the area. He introduces me to the old woman living next door, who says her children, when they were young, used to play with the children from Mrs Walsh's house. Shaking her hand, I can't help feeling a connection with my former self, all those years ago.

Later that evening, the man sends me a photograph of a

black-and-white picture he retrieved from the attic, a portrait of a young woman he believes is Mrs Walsh. In a dark dress and pearl necklace, the woman stares enigmatically at the camera, her lips sealed, a sadness about her.

I hadn't expected to find that my foster mother was still alive, but there was still hope of locating her family members. Google searches turned up nothing on her, though there was mention of a family member living for a time at the address where I was reared. On social media, I came across a photo of a Mrs Walsh in middle age, who lived on the right street in Bray. But when I contacted the person who had put the picture online, he said this was a different woman. The woman I was looking for, he believed, was known as 'English Mrs Walsh' due to her London background. Her husband, also long deceased, worked as a groundsman in a large estate nearby. She was, my correspondent assured me, 'one lovely lady'.

I posted messages about my search on a number of local bulletin boards. Within days, I received a response from a circumspect young woman asking why I was seeking information about Mrs Walsh. I told her the outline of my story, explaining how I had recently learned of the years I spent in Bray with a woman bearing this name.

My contact confirmed that Mrs Walsh, whose first name was Imelda, was her grandmother. She had died more than twenty-five years ago.

The woman asked her father about me, but he had no recollection of a baby coming into the house at the time I was there. I mentioned the trip to Butlin's when, according to my file, Mrs Walsh had to come back early because I was crying so much, while 'the boys' stayed on. Perhaps that might stoke some memories?

Sadly, it didn't. Her father had 'absolutely no recollection' of me being in his mother's care, the woman replied after checking again with him, and neither did an older brother. A younger brother, closest in age to me, had died years before.

The woman and her dad wished me well with my search but said they could not be of any more help because he had no memory of me.

I was left with an odd feeling of disappointment. While thoroughly understanding how people forget events from their childhood – there are large gaps in my own recollection – it felt strange to be not-remembered in this way. A non-person again; the boy who wasn't there.

57

As a child, I played with puppets a lot. It wasn't just that they provided much-needed company for an only child with a vivid imagination. In my play, I assigned each puppet a specific role. There was always a shy puppet trying to find his voice, and a baby puppet struggling with the demands of two adult puppets. One puppet was forever packing his bags, preparing to leave home, while another was already flying around the world and climbing high peaks.

Each puppet was a version of me, I can see now, as I struggled to untangle my identity from confused roots. There was Lonely Me, Isolated Me, Adventurous Me, and many others. Any sense of unease or rebellion I felt was being channelled into my painted papier-mâché friends.

My father helped me create a troupe of these hand-puppets, using leftover newspapers and glue. Working together at a paint-stained table in the garage he used as a workshop, we formed each head by gluing successive layers of newspapers around a disused light-bulb. Once a layer was in place, we put it out to dry in front of the SuperSer gas heater. Then we affixed another layer, and a third after that.

The more layers we coated on the bulb, the more solid the head of the puppet became. In later layers, we shaped the paper to make features – eye-sockets, ears, lips. The character of the puppet grew before our eyes.

I think of myself having been created in a similar fashion, layers of youthful experience accreting to form my basic character. My personality, what makes me different, was shaped by interactions within and beyond my adoptive family. Yet at the heart of my being, around which character and personality grew, lay a darkness, a mystery space.

To finish making a puppet, the glass bulb at its core had to be removed, by banging the head we had created on the table. It was a tricky task: too soft a knock, and the bulb remained intact; too hard, and the entire head might break. It was easy enough to extract the metal cap and filament but the challenge was to shatter the bulb sufficiently to allow the glass fragments to be removed safely.

Most times, Dad managed to apply the right amount of pressure to shatter the glass, which he then scooped out with gloved fingers. Then we could get on with painting the puppet, and dressing it in clothes Mam ran up from leftover fabric.

It has taken me many years, and a few knocks, to break open the core of my existence, just like Dad and I used to shatter the core of each puppet to get it working. The contents have finally spilled out, in pieces that will never be put back together. But at least I now understand this core of nature within me, around which the nurture of my adopted years burnished my character.

What does it mean to be adopted? I find myself returning to this question more frequently as I get older. I'm playing a game of catch-up, I suppose, having avoided the subject for so long.

All adoption is a form of lottery, where children are taken from their natural environment – the nurture and support of at least one of their birth parents – and transplanted into another family. The process of selecting the adoptive family might be long and arduous, but the move remains highly random. Intentions are usually good, but history shows the reality can be tainted by malign factors – religious zealotry, the influence of money, human shortcomings, sometimes just bad luck. A process said to be in the interests of the child can end up functioning more in the interests of the adults involved.

In Ireland, children usually end up materially better off – or at least no worse off – than they might have been if adoption had not taken place. The process places a heavy emphasis on the financial means and stability of applicants. Screening ensures that prospective adoptive parents are likely to be better off and healthier than the general population. I recall one friend's application to adopt being rejected after he was seen smoking on the street.

However, material betterment is not the same as spiritual

betterment. A richer child is not necessarily a happier child. There are so many variables involved in raising someone; so many outcomes are possible.

Some adoptions end badly, but this happens in regular families too. When things go seriously wrong, the adopted status of the child is often highlighted, giving rise to a form of cognitive bias that distorts the overall picture.

Mam and I were mismatched, I can see that now. We were both strong, ambitious personalities, but she was denied an outlet for her talents while I was given every chance to learn and develop. Ironically, the more she drove me to succeed, the more she pushed me away from her. In another universe, I would have been apprenticed to Dad and become a fourth-generation painter and decorator. Instead, I sucked up all the learning I could, rejected the traditional world of my parents and left Ireland as soon as it was possible to do so.

I haven't come across any substantial research on the success or otherwise of adoption in Ireland. After more than seventy years of legal adoption, we simply don't know whether it 'works' overall – however that might be measured. One reason is the secrecy that attached to adoption for so long. There is also the fact that adoption was effectively privatised in the hands of religious agencies for years, with minimal state involvement or external accountability. The administrative records of these agencies remain closed.

Too often today, adoption stories are treated as a sort of treasure hunt. Reunions between adoptees and birth mothers have become a staple of prime-time television. We think that finding out what happened when a person was adopted – tracing their birth parent, for example – will make everything clear. In true fairy-tale style, everyone involved is expected to live happily ever after.

I haven't located everyone involved in my creation and upbringing and I haven't solved some of the mysteries therein, but I do have a better understanding of the environment in which events unfolded. I'm done with the what-ifs.

None of this changes the fact that as an adoptee, I will always feel different. My birth mother carried me for nine months, and then my care was handed over to others. I will always bear that vaguely delineated sense of loss that results from this separation from my birth mother. Even if I don't look different from those around me, I will always feel different. The trauma is inherent, though largely hidden. In my case, there was yet more trauma when I was moved from one foster care situation to another before landing with my adoptive parents and finding stability.

I have found the search recounted in this book cathartic. By learning more about what happened before, during and after my adoption, I know so much more now about the actions and motivations of my parents and caregivers. Even the actions of the social workers have proved fascinating.

In the summer of 2025, I tracked down the woman who had arranged my adoption. Now aged ninety-three, almost blind and living alone, she was happy to talk about her decades arranging almost 1,000 adoptions through the agency.

'I am a believer,' she told me near the end of our chat, 'and I say to the Lord: I hope anything I did at the time was for the right reasons. But what was it all about? *Níl fhios agam* [I don't know]. We thought we were doing the best at the time. But maybe we weren't.'

58

I am a lucky man.

I survived a life-threatening fall from the Alps and, eight years on, I have substantially recovered from my injuries. There was the occasional reverse, among them an eye problem – thankfully short-lived – that I developed six months after the accident. Those troublesome bouts of back spasm whose origin was impossible to trace are now rare. Just about every day, I feel a dull ache internally that serves as a reminder of what happened on the mountain, but I can happily live with that.

I have relearned my limits and retain a rich and active life. Last year, I completed the Camino Francés, an 800-kilometre walk across northern Spain. I am back running regularly again, at a more modest level than before. Recently, I completed a short triathlon.

It could all so easily have gone another way, I know. Another bump on that Alpine slope might have severed my spinal cord, or caused my head to be bashed irredeemably. A similar accident in a more remote location, and hypothermia might have done for me. I had the good fortune to be rescued promptly by helicopter, treated immediately by expert paramedics and operated on in a specialist clinic that had the expertise to perform the complex surgery I required.

Recently, I came across Salman Rushdie's account of surviving a horrific knife attack in 2022. A combination of luck, surgical skill and loving care gave the author 'a second chance' in life, he wrote in his memoir *Knife*. Having 'beaten the odds', he asked himself the same question I did, the same question asked by anyone who gets a chance to cheat death: What do you do with your second opportunity? How do you use it?

Rushdie vowed to live life and to love as fully as he could. So did I, but the accident, once I survived it, also prompted a re-evaluation of my life, as I have set out in these pages. Not many people get the opportunity to be jolted into action in such a forceful manner. Life, I say, cleaving to one of my favourite clichés, is not a rehearsal. My accident was life-changing, but not just in the obvious way. It forced me to confront issues I had been ignoring hitherto, and set me on a healing voyage of discovery into my own identity. Lying on the mountain, I got to ask myself what I wanted from this life; by surviving, I got, in Raymond Carver's words, a second chance 'To call myself beloved, to feel myself/beloved on the earth'.

Self-discovery is the job of a lifetime. The search for my beginnings has taken years and, even then, questions remain unanswered. And yet I don't feel disappointed. Isn't it more about the journey than the arrival at a destination; more about whom you meet along the way than what you find at the end; more about how you change than about your reform expectations of other people?

I *have* changed on this journey. All my life I carried an anger, though it took years for me to realise this. Anger is an energy, as the song goes, which can be channelled to good purpose. But it can also be destructive. It seldom ages well.

I understand now that my anger is probably rooted in early experiences: the turmoil of those first weeks; the trauma of being passed from one mother to another, and then another; buried anxiety over what might have happened during the unrecorded sections of my past. All of these experiences drove my inner critical voice and led me to question the world I grew up in; first at home and then more broadly in the world. It helped make a journalist of me, but it also steered me into dangerous places, including the mountain I fell down.

'Most people's problems in this world with mental health come from the fact that they've lost connection with any fire in their bellies, in their own fundamental will to live,' the psychologist Dr Tony Bates told me once. His observation has stayed with me.

In any case, little can be done now to undo this ferment, other than to place it in a proper context. Yes, I have experienced adversity, as have many others, but I have been more than lucky in the circumstances of my upbringing and the friends who have enriched my life.

Having tracked their journeys through life in such detail, I have the overwhelming sense of the important adults in my early years looking out for me as best they could. They were ordinary, loving people, working within the resources available to them, the limits imposed by their times and the constraints of their physical and mental health. Whether present or absent, temporary or permanent, my birth, foster and adoptive mothers supported me to the best of their ability.

It hurts that I do not know everything that happened to me in those early, critical years. It also hurts that I never got to meet my genetic father, who may not have known of my existence when it mattered, before I was born. Yet there is balm in having discovered so much, and having come so close to knowing him. Sometimes things are just not meant to be. Now, after the years of searching, I allow myself to heed Søren Kierkegaard's advice that 'life is a mystery to be lived, not a puzzle to be solved'.

The past really is a foreign country, as the quote goes, where things are done differently. That, I think, is what I have learned from this story. Humans are imperfect. Societies dictate what we do and how we live our lives. Few of us possess the strength and bravery needed to swim against the tide. Life takes its toll, and we fray. Judgement can be clouded by so many factors: adverse experiences, passion, poverty, religious zealotry. People try to do their best, yet their best will probably never be good enough when judged by later generations.

I received love in my adoptive home – intense, undemonstrative, flawed love sometimes – and in time I learned to give love in return. Tears often fell, and apologies were made for wrongs perpetrated as hugs were exchanged. Not perfect, but at least the hugs happened.

Love threads the different elements of my story, I can see now. That love was at times strained, tainted, distant or went unexpressed, but it was there. It had the power to endure and to sustain, despite the broken lives, the frustrated ambitions and the severed connections that occurred.

I still wake from dreams thinking I am up there on the mountain. Time has frozen. Once again, I am suspended in space. The abyss below waits for me. I have just this brief moment before everything changes.

That day, I know, I should have been carrying specialist equipment for the icy snow conditions that prevailed at the top of the climb – crampons, rope and an axe. But I was excited to be back in the high mountains after a long break while my children were growing up. Surrounded by jagged Alpine peaks, under clear blue skies, it felt great to be alive. But my adrenaline rush had ebbed by the end of the day, when I was probably more tired than I had realised. I was out of practice, and my guard slipped. I made a wrong decision and paid heavily for it.

Time unfreezes. Today, there is no chasm for me to fall into. I roll out of bed and plant my feet on solid ground. I reach out a hand and steady myself on the bed-post. With one clean movement, I stand up and go live my life for another day. Older, wiser. A survivor.

Acknowledgements

I apologise in advance for repeating the oft-made comparison between writing books and delivering children. Yet given the subject matter, it does feel as if I have given birth to this book, my gender notwithstanding.

Being a man, my delivery was pretty slow. I was a journalist for many years, well used to the demands of meeting a deadline, but I was not in the habit of writing about myself in any detail, perhaps because I was fearful of where that might take me. As a result, the production of this book has taken much longer than the traditional nine-month gestation.

Many people helped me along the way. Friends, especially Alison and Eleanor, helped me clarify what the book was about at an early stage when my thoughts remained jumbled.

Journalistic colleagues, notably Patsy, Martin, Ronan and Harry, tutored me on the ways of the publishing industry to great effect.

Dr Tony Bates was generous with his time and helped to refine my thinking, particularly on that crucial period of my life when I was separated from any parent.

I am thankful to adoption advocates for giving me the benefit of their knowledge. Dr Claire McGettrick proofed sections of the text outlining the history of adoption legislation as it related to birth information and tracing, and Patricia Carey gave me the benefit of her wisdom and experience. Catriona Crowe was, as ever, splendidly eloquent and encouraging.

Members of my various families helped fill in gaps in my recollection of long-past events and, in some cases, corrected my memory when it proved errant; thanks to Máire, Rita and Teresa and also to Maria and Annette.

The book begins with an account of an accident that befell me in the Bavaraian Alps in 2017. Each of the three schoolfriends who were with me that day – Paul, Paul and Joe – were affected in their own way. I am grateful for their steadfast friendship and support to this day.

Writing this book was a largely solitary exercise, made easier by the assistance provided by archives and other institutions. In particular, I would like to thank staff at the Dublin Diocesan Museum, the Garda Museum, the National Library of Ireland, Rathmines Library and the archive of the Adoption Authority of Ireland.

I had the good fortune to have Jonathan Williams as my agent. His approbation for an earlier draft helped drive me to complete the manuscript.

Thanks to Hachette for agreeing to publish this memoir. That gave me the privilege of working with publisher and editor Ciara Considine, who followed up her initial enthusiasm for the book with considered suggestions for improving it. Thanks to Ciara, many darlings were harmed in the process. I am grateful for the attention she has given this project, and for the encouragement she has provided. I owe a debt too to Aonghus Meaney for spotting so many of my often painful chronological and geographical infelicities during copy-editing.

To our children, Ella, Rosa, Tana and Luca, I am forever grateful for filling our home with your noisy, busy lives and for filling our hearts to bursting. Finally, I would like to thank Dee for believing in me from the start. Your unstinting support gave me the confidence to confront issues I had been avoiding for years to see this project to completion. I will always be in awe of you.

pcullenmedia@gmail.com

Bibliography

Researching this book led me to read widely on adoption, trauma and related subjects. While it was never my intention to write an academic work, I include the following bibliography as a guide to references in the text and an aid for the interested reader.

Abramson, Harold J., *Issues in Adoption in Ireland* Economic & Social Research Institute, 1984.

Adoption Authority of Ireland, Original Adoption Societies Register, 1953–2005. Accessed at AAI Archive, 22 April 2025.

—Annual Reports

—Facsimile administrative records regarding CPRSI's registration and accreditation, December 1952–October 1992. Accessed at AAI Archive, 22 April 2025.

—Reflections on the Irish Domestic Adoption Process 1952–2022 (including contributions from Anne Ronayne, Laetitia Lefroy) 2024.

—Personal Cúnamh records. Obtained from AAI 2023–25.

Barrett, Monsignor Cecil, *Adoption: The Parent, the Child, the Home*, Clonmore & Reynolds, 1952.

Bates, Tony, *Breaking the Heart Open: The Shaping of a Psychologist*, Gill Books, 2023.

Bowlby, John, *Maternal Care and Mental Health* World Health Organization, 1951.

—*Child Care and the Growth of Love*, Penguin Books, 1953.

—*Attachment* series (three volumes) Basic Books, 1969–79.

Carver, Raymond, 'Late Fragment' in *A New Path to the Waterfall*, Atlantic Monthly Press, 1994.

Cúnamh, *All Born Under the One Blue Sky: Irish People Share their Adoption Stories*, Pigeonhouse Books, 2013.

Doyle, Paddy *The God Squad*, Transworld Publishers, 1989.

Earner-Byrne, Lindsey, *Mother and Child: Maternity and Child Welfare in Dublin, 1920s-1960s*, Manchester University Press, 2007.

—'The Boat to England: An Analysis of the Official Reactions to the Emigration of Single Expectant Irishwomen to Britain, 1922–1972', *Irish Economic and Social History* Vol. 30 (2003), pp. 52-70.

Elliott, Sue, *Love Child: A Memoir of Adoption, Reunion, Loss and Love*, Vermilion, 2005.

Ferriter, Diarmaid, *The Transformation of Ireland 1900-2000*, Profile Books, 2004.

Flynn, Mannix, *Nothing to Say*, Ward River Press, 1983.

'Forced Adoption: '"I was abducted and my baby kidnapped" under British-Irish scheme', ITN News, 6 May 2025. www.itv.com/news/2025-05-05/i-was-abducted-and-my-baby-kidnapped-under-british-irish-scheme.

Garrett, Paul Michael, 'The abnormal flight: The migration and repatriation of Irish unmarried mothers', *Social History*, 2000, Vol. 25, No. 3, pp. 330–344. www.tandfonline.com/doi/abs/10.1080/03071020050143356.

—'The hidden history of the PFIs: The repatriation of unmarried mothers and their children from England to Ireland in the 1950s and 1960s', *Immigrants and Minorities*, 2000, Vol. 19, No. 3, pp. 25–44. www.tandfonline.com/doi/abs/10.1080/02619288.2000.9974998.

—'The "Daring Experiment": The London County Council and the discharge from care of children to Ireland in the 1950s and 1960s', *Journal of Social Policy*, 2003, Vol. 32, No. 1, pp. 1–18. https://www.cambridge.org/core/journals/journal-of-social-policy/article/abs/daring-experiment-the-london-county-council-and-the-discharge-from-care-of-children-to-ireland-in-the-1950s-and-1960s/5428CD08EFF9E43144219028BF1D8A4A.

—'Unmarried Mothers in the Republic of Ireland', *Journal of Social Work*, 2016, Vol. 16, No. 6, pp. 708–25. journals.sagepub.com/doi/abs/10.1177/1468017316628447.

—'Fleeing Ireland: social exclusion and the flight of Irish "unmarried mothers" to England in the 1950s and 1960s', *Social Work and Irish People in Britain: Historical and contemporary responses to Irish children and families* Policy Press, 2004.

Good, Father James, Audio interview with Maurice O'Keeffe 2005 Irish Life and Lore/irishlifeandlore.com.

—'Priest: We were fairly sure nuns weren't obeying laws'. Interview with Niamh Horan, *Sunday Independent*, 8 June 2014.

Harris, Anne M., *Unspoken*, Anne M. Harris, 2020.

Kelly, Ruth J.A., *Motherhood Silenced: The Experiences of Natural Mothers on Adoption Reunion*, Liffey Press, 2005.

Lee, J.J., *Ireland, 1912–1985: Politics and Society*, Cambridge University Press, 1989.

Lifton, Betty, *Journey of the Adopted Self: A Search for Wholeness,* Basic Books, 1995.

Litster, Alice, *Unmarried mothers, in Great Britain and at home. 8 May 1948. Implementation of the children's acts 1945–51*, National Archives, Clandillon Papers.

Milotte, Mike, *Banished Babies: The secret history of Ireland's baby export business*, 2nd edition, New Island Books, 2012.

Mother & Baby Homes Commission, Final Report 2020. Department of Children, Disability and Equality, January 2021.

Palmer, Angela & O'Brien, Valerie, 'The Changing Landscape of Irish Adoption: An Analysis of Trends (1999–2016)', *Child Care in Practice*, www.ucd.ie/socialpolicy workjustice/newsandevents/angelapalmerandvalerie obrienpublisharticleinchildcareinpractice. Published in 2018.

Palmer, Caitriona, *An Affair with My Mother*, Penguin Books, 2016.

Redmond, Paul Jude, *The Adoption Machine: The Dark History of Ireland's Mother and Baby Homes and the Inside Story of How Tuam 800 Became a Global Scandal*, Irish Academic Press, 2018.

Roper, Mark, 'After the Fall' *Bindweed* Dedalus Press, 2018.

Rushdie, Salman, *Knife: Meditations After an Attempted Murder*, Jonathan Cape, 2024.

Sixsmith, Martin, *Philomena*, Pan Books, 2013.

Stewart, Colleen Mary, 'A study of the infrastructure and legislation for adoption in Ireland *c.*1911–1971'. Thesis for the degree of PhD. Department of History, National University of Ireland Maynooth, October 2013.

Tugendhat, Julia, *The Adoption Triangle: Searching and Uniting*, Bloomsbury, 1992.

Van Es, Bart, *The Cut Out Girl: A Story of War and Family, Lost and Found*, Penguin Books, 2018.

Verrier, Nancy Newton, *The Primal Wound: Understanding the Adopted Child*, Gateway Press, 1994.

Whyte, J.H., *Church and State in Modern Ireland 1923–1979*, Gill & Macmillan, 1980.

Winterson, Jeanette, *Why Be Happy When You Could Be Normal?*, Grove Press, 2015.

Archives and Libraries

Adoption Authority of Ireland Archives

Dublin Diocesan Archives

Garda Museum

National Archives of Ireland

National Library of Ireland

Rathmines Library